Two Patterns of Rationality in Freud's Writings

Two Patterns of Rationality in Freud's Writings

Steven E. Goldberg

The University of Alabama Press

Tuscaloosa and London

Copyright © 1988 by
The University of Alabama Press
Tuscaloosa, Alabama   35487
All rights reserved
Manufactured in the United States of America

Library of Congress Cataloging-in-Publication Data

Goldberg, Steven E., 1951–
    Two patterns of rationality in Freud's writings.

    Originally presented as the author's thesis (Ph.D.—DePaul University, 1986).
    Bibliography: p.
    Includes index.
    1. Psychoanalysis.   2. Psychoanalysis and philosophy.   3. Freud, Sigmund, 1856–1939—Contributions in philosophy.   I. Title.
BF175.G647   1988   150.19′52   87-5821
ISBN 0-8173-0366-9

British Library Cataloging-in-Publication Data is available.

To Katherine

It may perhaps seem to you as though our theories are a kind of mythology. . . . But does not every science come in the end to a kind of mythology?

—Freud

The speech of man is like embroidered tapestries, since like them this too has to be extended in order to display its patterns, but when it is rolled up it conceals and distorts them.

—Themistocles

Tick is a humble genesis, tock a feeble apocalypse.

—Frank Kermode

Contents

Acknowledgments

I am indebted to my colleague Martin Kalin for his painstaking review and incisive criticism of my work. Stanley Martens, who offered helpful and perceptive comments on an earlier draft, deserves thanks as well.

l also wish to acknowledge the DePaul University Research Council for a generous competitive research grant that enabled me to complete this book during the 1986–87 academic year.

I dedicate this study to my wife, Katherine Goldberg. Only she can know the extent of my gratitude for her encouragement and support.

Two Patterns of
Rationality
in Freud's
Writings

Introduction

Freud and Philosophy

Long exiled from academic psychology, Sigmund Freud has since found a home in textual criticism, linguistics, and historical studies. He has been portrayed as an exegete of the mind whose deciphering method originated in the Jewish mystical tradition; as a cryptobiologist who cloaked the discoveries of Ernst Haeckel and Charles Darwin in the terminology of his "revolutionary" science; as the author of a quest story whose journey took place in the underworld of the mind; and as a humanist who tried to rescue the myth of the soul from the encroachments of mechanistic science. Interpretations of Freud are as numerous and varied as the volumes that have inquired into his life, his method, and his evolving theory of human nature.[1]

Although Freud has not yet secured a place in philosophy, it is in light of the philosophic tradition that an understanding of him is pursued here. With few exceptions, recent philosophers have found Freud worthy of discussion not because he has advanced debate concerning the possibility of a science of humankind but, on the contrary, because his theories are symptomatic of the logical errors and conceptual confusion so badly in need of philosophical analysis. Papers unkind to Freud gen-

erally argue either that psychoanalysis cannot meet the formal
requirements of scientific explanation—notably, the falsifi-
ability of hypotheses—or that his naive realism blinds him to
the dangers inherent in reifying the mind as an archaeological
site whose relics can be excavated and plainly observed.[2] In the
first instance psychoanalysis is assailed for its inability to free
the experimenter from the experiment; in the latter, it is ad-
monished for its failure to acknowledge the contribution of the
knower to the known.

I agree that philosophic issues can be located in Freud's writings that he never detected or systematically developed. This
does not imply, however, that he was unreflective or naive.
Newton was a scientist, not a philosopher, but it would be difficult to name another intellectual figure who exerted a greater
influence on modern philosophy. Freud has not directly influenced the thinking of contemporary philosophers as Newton
shaped Kant's, but his bold ambition to pioneer a science of
humankind has provoked fundamental questions regarding the
powers of understanding, the kinship between reason and desire, the workings of the mind, and the mutability of human
nature. Unfortunately, those who have dismissed Freud for his
failure to subject psychoanalytic claims to experimental or predictive tests have not scrutinized the underlying assumption of
the methodological unity of the sciences. Is the study of the
historical past analogous to observation of the natural present?
Can the methods of natural science be transferred to the study
of human agents whose intentions and motives may be comprehended in narratives which connect contingent episodes of
individual lives?

The widely divergent readings of Freud's work and the displacement of psychoanalytic concepts from psychology into
other disciplines should make us wary of intellectual imperi-
alism. My interest in interpretation as a prominent theme in
Freud's theory mirrors the very issues that arise in the act of
reading his texts: how a person's ideas mesh with the story of
his or her life; how different readings of the same text produce
conflicting interpretations that cannot be systematically resolved; how every theory involves the selection of events or

episodes that appear significant to the interpreter; and, finally, how one cannot merely "read off" the text of a life but must "read into" it to discern its meaning and truth. For Freud, these issues crystallized around the powers of memory and the psyche rendered in the form of a story or narrative. These philosophically rich concepts—memory and narrative—will guide my inquiry into Freud's retrospective science of humankind. My principal claim is that the unfolding story of psychoanalysis displays an unresolved conflict between two patterns of rationality, one associated with Galileo's model of deductive explanation, the other with the comprehension or telling of stories. By reading Freud's work as a sustained meditation on rationality—in the sense of both a method of inquiry and a distinguishing feature of human nature—we can see more clearly not only his hidden philosophical commitment but also its implications for the study of humankind.

Two Patterns of Rationality

The story to end all stories was authored in the Enlightenment and its plot sketched by Comte: religion in the form of stories, then philosophy in the form of metaphysics, and the denouement—science with its exact methods. In his *Discourse on Method*, Descartes conceded that "the delicacy of fiction enlivens the mind . . . and the famous deeds of history ennoble it."[3] But in the end he concluded that history and romance—indeed all stories of human life—are prescientific and characteristically distort the truth. "Fiction makes us imagine a number of events as possible which are really impossible, and even the most faithful histories, if they do not alter or embroider things to make them worth reading, almost always omit the meanest and most illustrious circumstances, so that the remainder is distorted."[4] Since Descartes's pronouncement, the scientific enterprise has found epistemologically unworthy the narratives of both possible worlds and the actual though remote world of the past.

Freud rehearsed Comte's story of the ascendancy of science

and fashioned his earliest speculation on the workings of the mind after mechanistic accounts of the natural world. More precisely, he sought to explain psychological behavior in terms of physiological mechanisms. "The Project for a Scientific Psychology" (1895), a posthumously published manuscript, represented Freud's first attempt to integrate his study of the neuroses into a general theory of the mind. In his own words, the "Project" set out to "furnish a psychology which shall be called a natural science . . . to represent psychical processes as quantitatively determined states of specifiable particles."[5] Although he soon abandoned the ideal of a purely quantitative model, upon the manuscript's completion Freud was satisfied that it stated the laws by which the experience of the past determines current mental activity: "Everything fell into place. The cogs meshed, the thing really seemed to be a machine which in a moment would run itself."[6] The machinery was governed by the unpleasure principle, according to which the mind always acts to reduce tension, to minimize unpleasure, which originates in the experience of early childhood.

Freud's speculation was prompted by his clinical experience, particularly by his detection of the origins of mental illness in his patients' remote past. Unlike most traumas, those infantile experiences behind neurotic illness were found to be less painful when experienced than when they were remembered. The "Project" proposed that the generation of quantities of somatic excitation at puberty altered the psyche's response to infantile sexual memories. Yet the representation of memory in the space of the cerebrum always had as its primary referent the patient's *interpretation* of his or her past, that is, the meaning, intention, and purpose embodied in highly individualized symptoms and (disguised) memories.

The coexistence in psychoanalysis of the language of mental energy and the unlocking of meaning has been aptly described by Paul Ricoeur as a "mixed discourse."[7] Under the term "energetics" he identifies Freud's dynamic approach to the nervous system or psyche, conceived as a field of conflicting forces which canalize quantities of excitation; mechanisms for the registration, storage, and retrieval of "mnemic images"; and the underlying principle of constancy (i.e., the nervous system tends to keep the level of excitation as low as possible). The method of interpretation, the deciphering of dreams and symptoms as the recollecting of meaning, earns Ricoeur's designation as "hermeneutics." Both modes of discourse proved integral to psychoanalysis; both continually jarred and jostled in a framework that could not make them fully compatible. Must desire and meaning be opposed (and yet conjoined) as body and mind? Without a metapsychology patterned after thermodynamics, does psychoanalysis shrink to a clinical technique devoid of scientific value or interest?

These questions can be addressed by returning to the competing conceptions of rationality implicit in Freud's mixed discourse. One restricts reason to the logical relations between the elements of a formal system; the other refers to the act of comprehension—whether achieved in science, literature, or history—as a purposive practice. As Stephen Toulmin suggests, the broader conception of rationality admits, indeed demands, historical pressures that disturb the ideal of a system of immutable truths.

> In science as much as ethics, the historical and cultural diversity of our concepts gives rise to insatiable problems only so long as we continue to think of "rationality" as a characteristic of particular systems of propositions or concepts rather than in terms of the procedures by which men change from one set of concepts and beliefs to another. . . . [Rationality] is an attribute, not of logical or conceptual systems as such, but of human activities or enterprises of which particular sets of concepts are the temporary cross-sections.[8]

The attractiveness of the restrictive account lies in the simplicity and rigor of a single form of explanation: the occurrence of an event follows by formal deduction (prediction) from statements about initial conditions and the application of general laws. Rendered in the form of a syllogism, we can say, (1) If X (initial conditions and general laws), then Y (event to be predicted; (2) X is present; (3) therefore Y must be present. This model of explanation, today called the "covering law model," reaches back to Galileo's science of dynamics or local motion.[9] It was the reduction of terrestrial motions to terms of exact mathematics which distinguished natural science from the humanities and whims of human judgment. Nature, Galileo wrote, acts only "through immutable laws which she never transgresses," and cares "nothing whether her reasons and methods of operating be or be not understandable by men."[10] Mathematical demonstration, exercised upon the order of nature, furnished the key to a universal science, a geometry of matter in motion. Departing from medieval metaphysics in which reality was stratified and teleologically ordered, Galileo and his successors comprehended the world purged of final causes and qualitative difference. By articulating laws that govern regularities in the empirical world, the Galilean model turned from questions concerning why a particular event occurs to how it occurs as the kind of phenomenon that ensues under specifiable conditions. Explanatory power was henceforth generated by the recognition of necessity in a well-confirmed law that connects an event with its antecedents.

Once the content of Freud's clinical findings exceeded his theoretical frame, the literal picture of the psyche as a nervous system gave way to an imaginary topography best described as a scene of action in which different roles or agencies would engage in ciphering (e.g., displacement, condensation) and deciphering. Models of the mind are, according to Freud, theoretical fictions which coordinate and systematize basic psychological concepts and the etiology of psychoneuroses. Such models are useful, indeed indispensable, provided that we are careful not to confuse the scaffolding with the edifice under construction.

I mention the evolution of Freud's models and theory to indicate that despite his turn away from neurophysiological theorizing, the *formal* demands of his fledgling science still derived from what I have called the Galilean model of explanation. An explanation, whatever its object, generally attempts to show (1) that X happened, (2) that X must have happened, and (3) why X happened. Requirements (2) and (3) are collapsed in the Galilean model. Historical accounts, on the other hand, explain *contingent* events, thereby meeting conditions (1) and (3) without promising the deductive necessity required by (2).

The conflict delineated by Ricoeur may now be restated in terms of the dual aims of psychoanalysis: to imitate the natural sciences as a body of laws to be applied universally to human behavior and to engage in historical inquiry as a means of reconstructing the genetic context of an individual's motives and actions. It remains to be seen precisely how historical narrative makes human action intelligible so that it, too, qualifies as a rational explanation. My line of thinking follows Arthur Danto's when he writes, "The difference between history and science is not that history does and science does not employ organizing schemes which go beyond the given. Both do. The difference has to do with the kind of organizing schemes employed by each. History tells stories."[11]

Danto's comment rejects—if only by implication—the conventional distinction between observational science and other forms of inquiry infected with interpretive bias. In defense of the scientific status of psychoanalysis, Heinz Hartmann once compared the metapsychological theory with the kinetic theory of gases. Neither molecular interactions nor the processes of the unconscious are directly perceived; yet we have direct confirmation of their efficacy in such observable effects as temperature and pressure in the former instance, symptoms and slips in the latter.[12] Ernst Nagel replied that if psychoanalysis functions as a theory comparable to the kinetic theory of gases, then it should satisfy the same logical criteria as other theories in natural or social science.[13] It must be capable of empirical verification by deducing determinate consequences from its propositions, and specific rules of procedure (i.e., "correspondence rules") should be unambiguously formulated to anchor the theory in definite facts. According to Nagel, psychoanalysis does not compare favorably with other theories because neither formal requirement can be satisfied by Freud: the correspondence rules are vague and the economic model little more than a metaphor; empirical verification is impossible because psychoanalysis supplies no objective procedure to decide between rival interpretations of behavior.

Ricoeur has not so much joined this debate as he has muted it by challenging the distinction upon which it rests.[14] To engage in conversation involves the observation of another person's words and actions, but this is far different from the researcher's observation of phenomena in a controlled laboratory setting. Ricoeur's rejection of Hartmann's analogy is not intended as an endorsement of Nagel but as a criticism of the logical positivist understanding of science adopted by *both* Hartmann and Nagel. No pristine observation or brute datum can be found because all experience is framed by the language we speak or, in the case of science, by the theory that frames all interpretation. Scientists do make observations independently of what they may expect or wish—subjectivity does not imply caprice—but they also constrain inquiry to answer questions of their formulation. If a kinship exists between the methods of psychoanalysis and physics, then it must be traced to their shared status as *interpretive* activities, a claim that both Nagel and Hartmann would deny.[15] These methods differ, in turn, with respect to the questions that they seek to answer, the kinds of phenomena they labor to explain.

The Case History and Narrative Explanation

Critics of psychoanalysis have either failed to appreciate the centrality of the case history—the narration of a unique, unrepeatable but intelligible sequence of events—or have begged the question by calling psychoanalysis unscientific without justifying their exceedingly narrow conception of what constitutes a science. Freud's clinical practice aimed at problem solving in a genetic context. Faced with a number of incongruities in the analysand's history, the analyst would direct his inquiry to the originating event of a neurosis, its development, the function of current symptoms in bringing about a certain end, or the symbolic meaning of a symptom or dream.[16] An explanation of this kind does not necessarily convey new information but redescribes it to fit apparently disparate phenomena into some organized and meaningful pattern of action. Psychoanalysis supplies a narrative which organizes piecemeal behavior into the comprehensible whole of an individual life. It does not conduct experimental research in a setting where independent investigators can repeat, check, and publicly control the reporting of data to see whether it conforms to a known law. Freud's own comparison of psychoanalysis with archaeology offers a clue to the affinity of the case history with the practice of history in its broad sense. The events of the past are accessible to the analyst only through *interpretive reconstruction* of dreams, associations, and symptoms characterized as "memory symbols." In an essay written on the etiology of hysteria in 1896, only one year after completing the "Project," Freud likened the investigation of the structure of the mind to an explorer's discovery of ancient ruins.

Imagine that an explorer comes in his travels to a region of which but little is known and that there his interest is aroused by ruins showing remains of walls, fragments of pillars and of tablets with obliterated and illegible inscriptions. He may content himself with inspecting what lies there on the surface and with questioning the people who live nearby. . . . But he may proceed differently; he may come equipped with picks, shovels, and spades, and may . . . make an onslaught on the ruins, clear away the rubbish and, starting from the visible remains, may bring to light what is buried. If his work is crowned with success, the discoveries explain themselves. . . . the many inscriptions, which by good luck may be bilingual, reveal an alphabet and a language, and when deciphered and translated may yield undreamed of information about the events of the past, to commemorate which these monuments were built. *Saxa loquuntur!*[17]

Although the analogy between psychoanalysis and archaeology is weakened by the spatial representation of the mind's ruins, it offers telling hints regarding the kind of inquiry or "organizing scheme" employed by Freud. Perhaps most important, the method of inquiry does not proceed from direct observation of an artifact's surface, nor from testimony of those who live in its vicinity. Observation of a neurotic's symptoms or a family

member's account of the source of the neurosis cannot "bring to
light what is buried." For that matter, the patient's own account
of his or her past, though useful as a source, cannot be accepted
uncritically. Ultimately, the stones—or memory symbols—
speak only in response to the analyst's-discoverer's reconstruction of the ruins through the deciphering of inscriptions, and
the various concepts which guide the analyst's inquiry are like
the tools in the archaeologist's kit: they enable him to "clear
away the rubbish" and discern the meaning amid the apparently random, unintelligible fragments.

Freud wrote in the *Interpretation of Dreams*, "What we describe as our 'character' is based on memory-traces of our impressions; and, moreover, the impressions which have had the
greatest effect on us—those of early youth—are precisely the
ones which scarcely ever become conscious."[18] The past inscribed in symptoms, slips, and dreams may form character
lines, but the true test of one's mettle is the resolve to acknowledge and interpret these traces in the harsh light of day. What
Freud meant can be illustrated by drawing upon an incident he
recalled from his own childhood. Beneath his beard, he bore a
scar but could not recollect the incident that had caused it.
When the memory finally surfaced during his self-analysis,
Freud reconstructed the scene that left its signature on his face.
He recounted climbing upon a stool "to get something nice"
when he lost his balance, caught his jaw against the door, and
suffered a bleeding wound. The memory was accompanied by
the thought, "It served you right." The accident's enduring
lesson appeared to be that the restless desire for something
nice—whether it beckoned in the cupboard of the kitchen, a
woman, or the mind—always has its dangers. But Freud did not
stop with this truism. As other memories of his childhood
gathered around the image of the cupboard, the scene ex-
panded to include the birth of his sister, the fear that his mother
would abandon him, and pain mixed with guilt when his peasant nurse, who taught him about heaven and hell, involved the
young Freud in a theft which led to her dismissal and imprison-
ment. As Edward Rothstein observes, the overdetermined symbol of the cupboard and its hidden memory trace (i.e., scar)

signified an emotional landscape populated with "threats of retribution, the dangers of exploration, the promise of femininity, and the experience of pain and fear."[19]

Freud maintained that some childhood memories may be so dense that interpretation would demand the presentation of an entire life history. Case histories are compressed biographies organized around meaningful symptoms, and the field of Freud's stories encompassed the symbolic actions and sufferings of patients whose intentions were unclear to them. The plot of the case history traces out connections that make human actions intelligible as the expression of individual character. But this connection is neither one of logical implication nor one of chronological sequence. The connection, as Stanley Hauerwas puts it, "seems rather designed to move our understanding of a situation forward by developing or unfolding it."[20] A historical narrative does not demonstrate the necessity of events but makes them intelligible by unfolding the story which displays their significance. It is important to note that, unlike a proposition or conclusion that can be detached from its argument, the meaning embodied in the narrative form of the story cannot be replaced by some other kind of account. Although a story may be said to have a point that can be stated independently of the narrative, we generally recognize that the point becomes platitudinous unless it returns us to the story for another reading. Only banal stories, the kind that do not bear a second reading, have a determinate moral easily separable from the story it unfolds. In Freud's stories, characters cannot be formulated prior to, or independently of, the narrative which exhibits its development.

Literary critics have exposed the crudity of the brand of psychoanalysis that identifies the meaning of a story with the neuroses and childhood complexes of either its author or characters.[21] I, too, find this sort of explanation sorely wanting and oddly opposed to Freud's *practice* of storytelling and interpretation in his own case histories. The clash between these two approaches to literary works—the application of psychoanalytic principles to complexes suffered by the author and the comprehension of plot as a network of significance—reflects

Freud's ambivalent attitude toward the aims and methods of psychoanalysis. I have suggested that the internal—and conceivably unconscious—conflict in Freud's mind springs from competing notions of rationality embedded in his work. And if character is shaped by how one attempts to resolve conflict, then the character of the man—of what lay beneath the beard— can be best understood by trying to decipher the traces that form his writings.

Earlier, I raised the question of whether desire and meaning can be harmonized in the context of psychoanalysis. The orthodox interpretation would lead us to say, "No, reason possesses no integrity of its own; all works of culture are by-products of channeled emotions that cannot otherwise be dissipated." So, for example, if we wish to understand DaVinci's art, we probe his latent homosexual tendencies and so forth. Ultimately, such inquiry will yield insights into the themes of his work and the impetus to his creative drive. The Cartesian view of the mind pictures reason and desire as antagonists. Philosophy itself has been identified with the exercise of reason untainted by passion or prejudice. The standard account of Freud preserves the dualism but makes desire the more prominent of the two. Humankind is still capable of great achievements, but they are no longer considered examples of transcendence or the natural operation of the mind. All that we call the work of civilization is said to result from ingenious compromises in which reason provides an outlet for irrational impulses.

This account of psychoanalysis is encouraged by Freud's metapsychology, his economic model in particular, but the relationship of reason to desire also receives a markedly different treatment in his writings. The identification of rationality with mathematical reasoning or experimental method not only severely limits the province of knowledge but it engenders as well an impoverished psychology, one which drives a wedge between the affairs of life and the theoretical activity of the mind. In classical philosophy, particularly Plato and Augustine, the *life* of the mind encompassed human identity. Desire and reason were not opposed but merged in the appetitive intellect, in the *desire* for order which gives determinate shape and meaning to one's life. Freud's case studies, I have said, are histories, but they are histories of a special kind. Case studies seek historical knowledge as an impetus to therapeutic change. The stories related by Freud plot the progress of the "talking cure," a dialogue between therapist and patient in which comprehension of the past increases self-understanding. Historians may add to their store of knowledge about a particular culture, institution, person, event, but analysands undergo therapy to enlarge and better define themselves. The analysand's sickness consists in a splintered identity, an avoidance or willful aversion to some significant part of his or her life that refuses to fade but cannot be faced directly without the assistance of an analyst.

Psychoanalytic knowledge is fundamentally *personal* knowledge. Interpretive reconstruction leads not only to enhanced understanding of particular episodes dating back to childhood but primarily to the restoration of "mental health," understood as the re-collection of scattered fragments of one's life in a unified whole. The activity by which therapy both discloses and unifies clinical material was termed "working through" (*Durcharbeitung*), a concept that reinforces the importance of the labor of reflection which moves us through a narrative from beginning to end. Psychoanalytic truths cannot be stated as detached definitions or propositions that derive from disinterested inquiry. They are woven instead into the text of a life for all who read into it: the layperson who peruses the published case studies, the analyst who deciphers the deformed language of the analysand's symptoms, and the analysand who struggles against forgetfulness to read his or her past in order to become the author of his or her present life.

Therapy and Confession

The therapeutic dimension of psychoanalysis has antecedents in the ancient doctrine of *anamnesis*, or recollection. Augustine's spiritual autobiography, *The Confessions*, charts the progress of his soul's ignorance to knowledge. Imaged in a series of "turns" (the *vert* family), his life unfolds as a configuration of desire. Kenneth Burke concentrates this conversion rhetoric in a single locution: "Because we have turned away (*aversi*) from God, we are perverted (*perversi*). We should return (*revertamur*), lest we be overturned (*ut non evertamur*)."[22] These misdirections and redirections of the soul are a far cry from the canalization of energy but are suggestive as a way of understanding the vacillation between acknowledgment and avoidance in the therapy hour.

The verbal action of therapy demands the narrative structure common to the case study and the *Confessions*. Augustine's autobiographical format enabled him to show how his evolving understanding of God was interwoven with his personal development. Written eleven years after the garden scene in which his sins were forgiven, the whole work turns, so to speak, on his conversion experience. As a bishop and priest, Augustine desired God and renounced his mundane thirst for carnal pleasure and fame, the temptations of his youth. But it would be a mistake to characterize the *Confessions* as the story of a man whose conversion is complete and now inspires his readers to follow the same path. The term *confessio* meant for Augustine both "accusation of self; [and] praise of God." As Peter Brown notes, Book X, the last in Augustine's personal narrative, was not the affirmation of a cured man but the "self-portrait of a convalescent."[23] Conversion did not represent a clear break with his past; instead, he insisted upon reorienting his life by recollecting the journey between the identities of "what I once was" (the impulsive young man) and "what I now am" (the chaste bishop). The seemingly chaotic past, he discovered, had been ordered entirely in terms that came to give meaning to his life. Correlative to the act of reading signs communicated by God was the act of writing as an expression of the soul's yearning for enlightenment: "I desire to do truth in my heart before thee, by confession: with my pen, before my witness."[24] As therapy for the soul, the *Confessions* revealed to Augustine the hidden order of his life and enabled him to redirect its continuing story as a longing for self-knowledge and union with the divine.

Freud's analysands did not write their own stories, and Freud himself penned them for publication only when the "conversion" or therapeutic cure seemed complete—although he would eventually confess, for reasons to be discussed, that analysis is necessarily an *interminable* struggle. The dynamics of psychoanalysis and Augustine's confessions are in other respects strikingly similar. Therapy promises a cure through speech, the exchange of words between analyst and analysand. This talking cure proceeds by forcing the analysand to interpret signs that are difficult to comprehend even though they may appear on the surface of his or her own body. Self-forgetfulness, the soul's turning away from itself, is purchased at the high price of psychic suffering and can be reversed only by recognizing what has been repressed and by tracing out its implications in the hope of redirecting the plot of one's life.

The parallels between Freud and Augustine do not extend, at least at first glance, to their methods of interpretation or the inflection of meaning disclosed by signs. After all, Freud renounced religion as an infantile fantasy, whereas Augustine maintained that only the "mature" or reflective soul could be receptive to the word of God. Even if Freud had no use for God, he could not do without what Kenneth Burke has called a "god-term." The design that we discern in our actions, the ingenious signs that call for interpretation, the simultaneous source and destination of our desire to know—these are all elements of Freud's negative theology of the unconscious. Like God, the unconscious is mute and timeless, inscrutable to man who lives in time and comprehends in speech. Yet the unconscious is also omnipresent, made evident to humankind through its signs or "instinctual representatives." Would it be reaching, finally, to suggest that Freud no less than Augustine was fascinated with the supernatural? Burke hints at what distinguishes Freud's "data" from that of the secular sciences when he writes, "In all such cases, where symbolic operations can influence bodily processes, the realm of the natural (in the sense of the less-than-verbal) is seen to be pervaded, or *inspirited,* by the realm of the verbal, the symbolic. And in this sense the realm of the symbolic corresponds to the realm of the 'supernatural.' "[25] The implications of a negative theology that eschews reference to God and finds the *Logos* rooted in instinctual life will be a central issue in the reflections that follow.

The Method and Outline of the Book

The philosophical themes previewed in this introduction—the dynamics of memory and forgetfulness, the interdependence of reason and desire, the irreducibly linguistic texture of purposeful behavior, the autonomy of historical discourse—all issue from the unresolved tension I have detected in psychoanalysis between Galilean and narrative modes of explanation. As mentioned, these competing models imply sharply opposed accounts of rationality. How we set out to study man—the methods we employ and the questions we ask—will have profound consequences for who or what is comprehended as the subject of a human science.

Although this book is exegetical and immersed in the details of Freud's thinking, my aim is to display and to assess conflicting philosophical positions in the evolution of psychoanalytic theory and method. I follow Freud's search for a suitable explanatory model by alternating between two perspectives: a close reading of explicitly philosophical themes in Freud's texts; and, from a vantage point outside psychoanalysis, scrutiny of philosophical presuppositions and implications that were never entertained or appreciated by Freud himself.

The sheer volume of Freud's corpus necessitates interpretive decisions concerning which texts are representative of the whole, as well as which are needed to pursue a particular line of reasoning. My own approach has consisted in perusing selected writings spanning Freud's career, including at least one that illustrates each of the psychoanalytic genres: the metapsychology, the case history, the summary or general introduction, and the technical papers on psychoanalytic method. Against this broad background, my own line of reasoning brings into relief the case history as an exemplar of narrative explanation. Generally, the writings that hold my interest cluster around the years between 1895 and 1920. The following are especially important for my purposes: the prepsychoanalytic "Unpublished Drafts" (1897–1902), *Studies on Hysteria* (1895), *The Interpretation of Dreams* (1899), *Totem and Taboo* (1912), "From the History of an Infantile Neurosis" (1918), and "Beyond the Pleasure Principle" (1920).

I have relied on Strachey's English translation of the *Standard Edition* except where key German terms have either ambiguous or controversial meanings. For example, Strachey's translation of *Seele* as "psychic apparatus" has a scientistic cast that conveys a meaning vastly different from the "soul" of traditional philosophy. Similarly, Strachey's questionable rendering of *Ich* as the Latinized "ego" fails to capture the common sense of "I" or of self-identity expressed in German parlance. These terms and others of philosophical importance (e.g., instinct, unconscious) are scrutinized in their original German context.[26]

The organization of the book for the most part parallels the chronological development of psychoanalysis. However, each chapter should be considered as a step in a sustained argument and not merely as historical commentary. The first chapter comes closest to what may be called a historical sketch, and its purpose is to trace the development of Freud's psychology of the neuroses as a response to the conceptual inadequacies of classical psychiatry. Trained in physiology and anatomy, Freud turned to these branches of medical science in hopes of solving the riddle of hysteria, an illness distinguished by physical symptoms without any organic basis. Freud, of course, eventually unlocked the secrets of hysteria by treating symptoms as signs to be interpreted through a talking cure. Here lies the beginning of the mixed discourse in which hermeneutics and energetics coexist, however uneasily, in Freud's mind. Although classical psychiatry could not accommodate his clinical findings, it continued to exert an influence on Freud's expectations for scientific objectivity and rigor. For example, the analogies by which he represented the workings of the mind borrowed conspicuously from the language of anatomy (spatial location = topography) and physiology (force = economic model). In the early years of his career, Freud thus struggled to find a framework that was both "scientific" and adequate to the distinctly linguistic and intentional qualities of his patient's behavior.

In chapter 2, I examine narrative explanation as the mode of comprehension appropriate to psychoanalysis. The psychoanalytic method is characterized as a species of historical inquiry, and the issues raised in this context are essentially those of historiography. How, for example, do we judge the success of narratives which claim to explain the origin and meaning of symptoms, parapraxes, and dreams? I reformulate this question in light of a threefold distinction: the events to be explained, the patient's report of those events, and the analyst's interpretation of the report in gaining access to the meaning of the pertinent events. Reconstruction proceeds through a series of interpretations of events which are themselves *events of interpretation* (e.g., childhood memories, fantasies, dreams). Consequently, the problem of validating a narrative explanation quickly opens up inquiry into how psychoanalysis can slip through the linguistic net in order to reach its object. Stated somewhat differently, how can the historical past be clearly demarcated from its purely verbal representation? The other epistemological issue connected with narrative explanation has been discussed briefly in the introduction. Here I am referring to the *logical* features of narrative as a putative science. The task, in this instance, is not to validate a particular interpretation, but to show in what sense any narrative qualifies as an *explanation*. Although both issues are formulated in chapter 2, this section brings into focus the structural features of psychoanalytic narrative. The case study is elucidated as a genre in light of such concepts as story, plot, fiction, and history. The latter part of the chapter deals at length with the question whether history can be raised to the level of a science. The problem of what qualifies as a method or criterion of science dovetails with the question of what counts as the subject matter of scientific study. I argue, in effect, that human subjectivity may be understood by narratives which exhibit the configuration of an individual life and that this mode of comprehension cannot be assimilated to the covering law model of explanation.

In the third chapter, I return to the issue of validation by asking how a case study can be assessed for its accuracy as a historical reconstruction of an individual's past. Narrative explanation, I have noted, makes each fragment of the patient's life intelligible by referring it to the context of meaning it either confirms or disconfirms. The success of the case study depends on continuity, closure, and the extent to which the pieces fit into a complete, aesthetically satisfying whole. This prescription for the case study echoes Aristotle's requirement that a dramatic narrative coincide with the *unity* of action that it conveys to the reader.[27] The analogy of the picture puzzle indicates how Aristotle's notion of internal necessity operated in Freud's own stories:

> Just as when putting together children's picture puzzles, we finally . . . become *absolutely certain* which pieces belong to the gap not yet filled . . . so the content of the infantile scenes [sexual seduction] proves to be an *inevitable* completion of the associative and logical structure of the neurosis; and only after they have been inserted does its origin become evident—one might say *self-evident*. [Emphasis mine.][28]

And yet the very "self-evident" piece needed to complete the puzzle proved to be a fantasy. Because language is far more elastic and ambiguous than a jigsaw puzzle, a close fit among the elements of a narrative does not guarantee their truth or accuracy. As a criterion for evaluating narrative constructions (fiction), "internal necessity" may sharpen our critical powers, but as a criterion for evaluating historical reconstructions (history), Aristotle's injunction arguably invites us to bias our explanations, to bend facts so that they fit a preconceived explanatory pattern. Donald Spence alerts us to twin dangers inherent in the talking cure: the power of suggestion in shaping the analysand's recollections and the analyst's tendency to place the desire for narrative closure before the explanatory requirements of empirical evidence. Psychoanalytic method arouses suspicion when, for example, a mediating link between apparently unrelated events—"castration threat," say—is introduced as a supposition but subsequently woven into the finished narrative and the analysand's memory as the analyst's empirical "discovery."

The issue, I try to show, is not simply the confusion of observational with theoretical language or of aesthetic criteria with explanatory demands. Ordinarily, we would test Freud's claims by matching the reconstructed text with evidence external to the intentional structure of experiences recollected or re-enacted by the patient. In other words, confirmation of what is depicted must come from outside, from the reality elucidated or dramatized by the plot of the case study. The question that now arises is essentially epistemological in nature: how can an interpretation be sustained if what is "external" to the interpretation is the "internal" domain called *psychical* reality, a reality populated with fantasies, associations, and corrupted memories. Against what standard do we assess our claims for accuracy when the "object" of investigation is intrinsically fantastic? Psychoanalysis, I argue, begins in the genre of the detective story, where every mystery has a single identifiable solution. The search for a trauma, a scene of crime, always found its quarry in Freud's early case studies. This positivistic confidence in the power of reason to uncover the truth was shaken by the indeterminacy of the origins of his patients' neuroses. In the crucial "From the History of an Infantile Neurosis," written between 1914 and 1918, Freud could not decide whether a decisive primal scene lay behind his patient's obsessional neurosis. Was the scene observed or invented? Did it, he finally asked, make any difference? The distinction between event (of interpretation) and interpretation (of event) becomes blurred, and Freud's detective story yields to a modernist fiction with multiple endings, his science to Werner Heisenberg's uncertainty principle. The difference that interests me is no less problematical: that between psychoanalysis as a science of fictions—one that understands the operation of fantasies and so forth—and a fictional science which fabricates to satisfy the analyst's desire for narrative closure.

Having shown how psychoanalysis qualifies as a species of historical inquiry, I propose in the fourth chapter that Freud also contributed to our understanding of how man exists as a uniquely historical being. The distance of the past from the perspective of the historian opens up the possibility of scepticism and error in historical reconstruction. In the context of the therapy hour, it is precisely the closeness of the past, its tyranny, that presents the greatest challenge to the analyst. Repression, symptom formation, and screen memories all betray the staying power of the past. Despite his emphasis on how we *are* our past, Freud has been attacked for his allegedly antihistorical stance, that is, for reducing diversity to uniformity, change to permanence, and ultimately history to psychology. After responding directly to the comments of Norman O. Brown and Philip Rieff, I turn to Freud's instincts theory in "Beyond the Pleasure Principle." Generally cited as an example of his biological determinism, this work has ostensibly little to recommend it as a meditation on history or historicality. However, read as an implicit metabiography, the essay merges hermeneutic and energetic modes of discourse in its model of the psyche as a "textual economy." The experience of reading a narrative from beginning to end offers a clue to how desire operates in its search for satisfaction. The binding of a plot which maintains suspense and delays the story's end resembles the binding of energy in the psyche's desire to die "in its own fashion." The repetition of the past, a key phenomenon in psychoanalytic theory, represents the projection of the end (death) from which we recollect the plot of life as a provisional whole. The formal unity of beginning, middle, and ending in stories derives from the fundamentally narrativizing—or historicizing—character of desire as the psyche stretches itself within the horizons of birth and death. By showing how "narrativizing" in Freud is consonant with Heidegger's conception of historicality, I attempt to bring the instincts theory within the proximity of a radical hermeneutics. Their shared interpretation of *finite* temporality as the key to historical existence invites a comparison of the death instinct (*Thanatos*) in "Beyond the Pleasure Principle" with being-towards-death (*Sein-zum-Tode*) as set out in *Being and Time*.

In the concluding chapter, I defend the primacy of both the case history as the central text of psychoanalysis and narrative explanation in Freud's interpretation of symbolic action. I then move from these exegetical concerns within psychoanalysis to broader philosophical issues which situate Freud's work but are not confined to it. My principal claim is that the Galilean model of rationality is inadequate both as a method for inquiring into human nature and as an account of what makes us human. An understanding of humankind cannot ignore the irreducibly historical, interpretive dimension of human experience. If narrative has a place in the comprehension of human action, can we go further and say that it provides a kind of explanation which qualifies as a science of humankind? Narrative, I conclude, ultimately serves the aim of self-knowledge through *anamnesis*, a moment of reflection that belongs to no particular science. This does not mean that psychoanalysis contributes nothing to our knowledge of human nature. On the contrary, by drawing Freud into dialogue with Plato, we may hear his voice in the conversation of philosophy and be grateful to him for retrieving a tradition that sets back the "sciences of humankind" a good two thousand years.

1

From Soma to Symbol: The Emergence of Psychoanalysis

Freud's reflections on the powers and limits of memory originated in his studies of hysteria in upper-middle-class Viennese women. Having observed that "neurotics suffer from reminiscences," he became convinced that memory symbols—the ciphering and deciphering of one's biographical past—are instrumental in the genesis and resolution of neurotic symptoms.[1] This preoccupation with the role of language and memory emerged in the context of a dispute between the anatomical and physiological approaches to psychiatry in the late nineteenth century; and by locating Freud's place in the debate, we can appreciate how his early psychology was colored by, and departed from, the thinking of his contemporaries.

As the title of this chapter suggests, the development of psychoanalysis can be traced from its beginnings in organic (i.e., anatomical) etiology to the understanding of neurotic symptoms as symbols that allusively signify important scenes from the patient's remote past. In the brief historical sketch that follows, I chart Freud's evolving theory and practice in three distinct but related stages: his tutelage under Charcot, whose demonstrations in the use of hypnosis urged upon Freud an ideogenic account of hysteria; the monograph on aphasia,

23

which stressed functional over anatomical considerations; and the influence of Breuer's treatment of Anna O. as a prototype for the talking cure and Freud's first intimation of transference. Throughout these stages of development, I emphasize the growing tension between medical and symbolic modes of inquiry that would vie for supremacy throughout his career.

Charcot and the Break with Anatomy

As a medical student at the University of Vienna in the early 1880s, Freud studied neuropsychiatry under Theodor Meynert, a prominent figure in the anatomical tradition. Meynert's research delineated various cerebral activities within distinct, localized areas of the brain. He believed that knowledge of the normal structure and function of the brain was necessary to gain an understanding of clinical symptoms, and he insisted that psychiatry, defined as the medical discipline concerned with diseases of the cerebral cortex, start from the anatomical facts.[2] These facts were discerned by performing autopsies on former patients in order to match symptoms with brain lesions.

Freud endorsed the anatomical approach to pathology and upon graduation from medical school accepted Meynert's offer to serve as his assistant at the Laboratory of Cerebral Anatomy. Under Meynert's tutelage Freud soon became adept at diagnosing symptoms as the effects of certain kinds of brain damage. In his *Autobiographical Study* (1925), he recalled how the combined observation of symptoms and knowledge of the nervous system enabled him "to localize the site of a lesion in the medula oblongata so accurately that the pathological anatomist had no further information to add."[3] With the help of Ernst Brücke and Meynert, Freud was awarded a fellowship to continue his work in Paris. In a letter to his fiancée, Martha Bernays, he excitedly announced his decision to pursue a career in brain anatomy: "I am tempted by the desire to solve the riddle of the brain: I think anatomy is the only rival you have or ever will have. . . . What I want, as you know, is to go to Paris . . . and have enough time to work on the brain."[4]

Jean Martin Charcot, the celebrated professor of anatomy and pathology at the University of Paris, earned his reputation at the dissecting table by elucidating brain lesions associated with nervous diseases, among them epilepsy and multiple sclerosis. Despite his emphasis on brain anatomy, Charcot insisted that dissection could not substitute for clinical observation. In a lecture delivered before the Académie des Sciences in 1882, he made the still stronger claim that anatomical research contributes *nothing* to the explanation of certain illnesses, notably hysteria.

> There still exists at the present time a great number of morbid states, evidently having their seat in the nervous system, which leave in the dead body no material trace that can be discovered. Various illnesses, among them hysterical, come to us like the Sphynx, which deny the most penetrating anatomical investigations. These symptomatic combinations, deprived of anatomical substratum, do not present themselves to the mind of the physician with that appearance of solidity and objectivity which belong to affections connected with an appreciable organic lesion.[5]

Psychiatrists in the anatomical tradition were undaunted by their failure to discover lesions underlying the symptoms of this curious disease. Far from questioning the adequacy of their orientation, they typically discredited hysteria as a disease precisely because anatomical evidence was lacking. Hysterical symptoms, in turn, were routinely attributed to intentional deception on the part of the patient. Charcot's clinical findings upset the conventional bias, demonstrating that the absence of an anatomical substratum is significant, since "hysteria is in fact a well-governed entity governed, in the same way as other morbid conditions, by rules and laws, which attentive and numerous observations permit us to establish."[6] To defend his position that hysteria is a legitimate disease which manifests clearly defined symptoms, Charcot still needed to answer the charge of simulation. He did so by indicating the discrepancy between symptomatic behavior and the physical signs attending merely feigned symptoms (e.g., tremors).

Charcot's lecture cast doubt on the existence of clear-cut anatomical lesions in hysteria, but the failure of autopsies to reveal
significant anatomical findings did not rule out the possibility
that such lesions might be present but difficult to detect.
Clinical evidence ultimately persuaded him that hysteria and
related neuroses do not have their origin in brain lesions and
cannot be understood anatomically. Although the symptoms of
hysteria follow definite rules, they do not conform to the anatomical organization of the nervous system. The paralysis of a
limb, for example, covers the area delimited by our ordinary
concept of an arm or leg rather than the area defined by the
actual distribution of sensory nerves.

As an alternative explanation, Charcot proposed that hysterical symptoms manifest a physiological or neurodynamic abnormality. He found in the phenomenon of hypnosis an important clue to the nature of the physiological mechanism
responsible for his patients' difficulties at the Salpêtrière Hospital. If hypnotic suggestion can induce a physical response
dissociated from conscious intentions and unrelated to any
physical disturbance, is it possible that paralysis and other hysterical symptoms arise in a similar fashion? Charcot tested his
hypothesis by using hypnotic suggestion to induce artificially
in a patient the same symptom of paralysis that was present in
another patient due to some physical trauma (e.g., railway accident). Anticipating Freud's psychogenic theory of symptom formation, Charcot suspected that all subconscious hypnotic suggestions were dependent upon a series of ideas somehow
isolated psychically from normal waking consciousness and residing in a separate region of the mind. Nevertheless, he maintained that hypnosis was at bottom a physiological abnormality
based upon dynamic changes throughout the nervous system.

The etiology of hysteria was traced to a physical trauma which
induces a hypnotic state in people who suffer from a *hereditary
predisposition* to the disease. The trauma, an event causing nervous shock or intense fear, leaves the hysteric susceptible to
hypnotic suggestion. The idea of paralysis, dissociated from normal consciousness, later materializes as an objective symptom.
From this account, Charcot derived the therapeutic technique he

was seeking. Hypnosis enables the therapist to penetrate the altered state of consciousness which was induced by the patient's spontaneous hypnosis at the time of the trauma. New suggestions can then be made to counter and expel the idea of paralysis, thereby ridding the patient of the debilitating symptom.

It must have been a rude awakening for Freud, whose study of the structure of the brain was just beginning, to hear Charcot proclaim that the work of anatomy was finished. The shock soon wore off, however, as Freud, himself spellbound by Charcot's demonstrations, became convinced that hysteria is a genuine disease with uniform symptoms, that hysterical symptoms behave as if they were ignorant of anatomy, and that hysteria is a hypnotic state, physiological in nature, occasioned by nervous shock in individuals predisposed to the illness.

Charcot's telling link between hysteria and hypnosis undoubtedly provided the stimulus to Freud's psychological theory and clinical practice. Yet it was not Freud but Hippolyte Bernheim who first saw the implications of hysteria as purely psychological. Bernheim discarded Charcot's explanation of hypnosis as a hereditary trait manifested in neuroses and argued instead that suggestion, operating independently of physiology, is sufficient to cause the symptoms associated with hysteria. Because all people are susceptible to suggestion—not just hysterics—and because differences in behavior can be traced to the influence exerted by ideas on the mind, Bernheim concluded that both the act of hypnotism and its effects should be explained ideogenically, as the consequence of conscious suggestions conveyed to the hypnotized subject.

As David Levin has noted, Freud vigorously defended Charcot's physiological model against both extremes: the anatomical model, which reduced all disorders to locatable physical disturbances in the brain, and the psychological model, which denied that physical occurrences of any kind contributed to hysterical symptoms.[7] The latter claim had particularly damaging consequences for Charcot's theory of hysteria. If hypnosis resulted from purely mental suggestions, then it could be argued that the symptoms were not genuine and had been falsi-

fied by the observer, who induced, intentionally or uninten-
tionally, the desired results. Charcot presumed that anyone
who could be hypnotized must be susceptible to hysteria; yet
he never tested his powers of suggestion on subjects who were
manifestly normal. If suggestion works upon the minds of patients and physicians alike, should it still be considered an abnormal physiological state? Was hysteria a matter of deception
after all, a ruse which the physician and patient performed for
each other's benefit?

Freud, of course, never entertained these possibilities and
while under Charcot's influence tried to rescue his mentor's
theory from critics who pronounced hysteria a chimera. In defense of Charcot, he cited the conformity of reports of uniform
stages of illness (cataleptic, lethargic, and somnambulic) and
classical symptoms (contractures, neuromuscular spasms)
which together demonstrated the existence of a legitimate
clinical type. Suggestion, Freud insisted, must be set in the context of hypnosis considered, not as a psychical phenomenon,
but as a physiological state: "The description of major hypnosis
offers symptoms which tend most definitely against their being
regarded as psychical. I refer to the increase in neuromuscular
excitability during the lethargic stage. . . . Anyone who has
seen this will inevitably assume that the effect must be attributed to physiological reasons or to deliberate training."[8]

Aphasia

Yet elucidation of "physiological reasons" for hysteria was
sketchy at best. For an understanding of the contribution physiological theory made upon the development of psychoanalysis,
we need to consider Freud's monograph On Aphasia (1891).[9]
Published several years after his first writings on hysteria and
hypnosis, this work offered a critique of anatomy as a model for
explaining the operations of the speech apparatus and onset of
aphasic symptoms. His principal argument was that general
functioning should take precedence over anatomical evidence.

An understanding of the normal activity of speech, Freud believed, required knowledge of the relationship between brain structure and its characteristic modes of operation; aphasia, in turn, should be understood as the consequence of dysfunction or lower levels of operation than normal within a given anatomical unit.

During the late nineteenth century, the theory of cerebral localization dominated the study of aphasia. Paul Broca demonstrated in 1861 that the loss of speech was due to a lesion in the frontal lobe, and in 1874 Paul Wernicke, a protégé of Meynert, associated another site in the brain with the loss of ability to comprehend spoken words. Correlating clinical disturbances of speech with anatomical abnormalities, these so-called "diagram makers" depicted the speech apparatus as the composite of a motor center (Broca's area), an auditory center (Wernicke's area), and association paths connecting the two centers. Although he acknowledged the presence of anatomical lesions in aphasics, Freud questioned the soundness of superimposing brain functions and the association of ideas on an anatomical map of brain structure. Against this atomistic division of the speech apparatus into separate centers for memory registration and storage and association paths for the coordination and retrieval of memories, Freud proposed a functional explanation that substituted physiology for anatomy. Specifically, he insisted that the association of ideas and their individual retrieval are functionally integrated so that normally all anatomical units participate in the comprehension and practice of speech. In his attempt to represent the unity of language in the workings of the nervous system, Freud replaced discrete local centers of functioning with a single, uniform mass of connecting fibers.[10]

If normal speech mobilizes all anatomical units in the speech apparatus, then a lesion would impair its general level of functioning rather than eliminate a discrete operation of speech or memory corresponding to the site of the lesion. And if malfunction forces the speech apparatus as a whole to operate at a deficit, then the clinical symptoms of aphasia must be attributed not to the location of the affected cells but to the magnitude of the damage suffered by the entire region of the brain that controls speech.

Following Hughlings Jackson, Freud argued that aphasia conforms to the principle of functional regression in which deteriorating language skills revert to a more primitive level of organization, thus reversing the sequence of language acquisition. Sophisticated language skills involve the substitution and combination of words to form propositions that suit the occasion of their utterance. These skills are the first to succumb to aphasia as the illness wrenches words from the linguistic context in which they originally conveyed meaning. Jackson thus distinguished "live" intentional utterances from those "dead," recurrent utterances that betray the loss of higher levels of functioning.

Although Freud's physiological speculation on aphasia lagged behind his nascent psychological account of hysteria, hindsight permits us to see how the two phenomena contributed jointly to the conceptual development of psychoanalysis.[11] Like the aphasic utterance, the hysterical symptom was regarded as a linguistic expression that, once isolated from its historical origins, lost its meaning and was doomed to repetition as pathological behavior. Freud was convinced that both aphasic utterances and hysterical symptoms could be illuminated by reconstructing the traumatic context in which they acquired significance. When he asked why a specific aphasic utterance was found, Freud would turn to the history of the syndrome for a specific event or affect that might supply an explanation. Similarly, the understanding of hysteria would require a historical mode of inquiry, a search in time for the "lost" words at the origin of the neurotic symptom.

The Case of Anna O.

The famous and now familiar case of Anna O. was the first example of the genetic method to arouse Freud's interest.[12] From December 1880 to June 1882, Joseph Breuer treated a young, intelligent woman who suffered from an array of symptoms which first appeared when she kept vigil at the bedside of her fatally ill father. During the period of treatment, Anna exhibited hysterical paralysis, disturbances of vision, and aphasic symptoms. Breuer discovered that her worsening aphasia abated when he suggested that she was hiding something from him. "When I guessed this and obliged her to talk about it," wrote Breuer, "the inhibitions, which had made any other utterances impossible as well, disappeared."[13] This practice of "chimneysweeping" improved her condition until the death of her father in April triggered a serious setback.

For more than a year, Anna experienced hallucinatory episodes which blended fantasies with memories of the earlier months of her illness and, more important, the period during which she nursed her father. Breuer discovered that once Anna had vividly recalled, in reverse chronological order, the events which surrounded the onset of the symptoms, the symptoms would disappear. From his clinical experience with Anna O., he formulated a new therapeutic technique. "Each individual symptom in this complicated case was taken separately in hand; all the occasions on which it had appeared were described in reverse order, starting before the time when the patient became bed-ridden and going back to the event which had led to its first appearance. When this had been described, the symptom was permanently removed."[14]

Although Breuer related the case to Freud at the time he was treating Anna O., Freud apparently showed little interest until his commitment to pathoanatomy was challenged by the clinical implications of Charcot's etiological connection between hypnotism and hysteria. Once Freud turned to the study and treatment of this puzzling neurosis, his imagination was excited by Breuer's pioneering study in which hypnosis elicited Anna's memories of the origin and genesis of the illness, thereby effecting a cure. Taking the case of Anna as the prototype for their new theory of hysteria, Freud and Breuer argued that the events which surrounded the first appearance of hysterical symptoms constituted not a physical shock but a psychical trauma causing intense fear and anxiety: "An experience which causes distressing affects—such as those of fright, anxiety, shame, or pain—may operate as a trauma of this kind."[15] Following Charcot, they held that the trauma produces an idea which is firmly planted in a second region of the mind that denies access to normal consciousness. The hysterical symptoms surface when the memory of the objectionable event is inhibited. Breuer and Freud also agreed that restoring consciousness of the source of the illness was a necessary but insufficient condition for successful treatment and cure. Therapy for Charcot involved the use of countersuggestion to bring the inhibited idea into association with fully conscious and normal trains of thought. However, Breuer and Freud found that it was also necessary that the patient "relive" the original emotional distress that accompanied the traumatic event. "Recollection without affect," they remarked, "almost invariably produces no result."[16] The talking cure consisted in reevoking the memory of the trauma and putting the affect associated with the memory into words.

Breuer recounted an incident which illustrates the last point. On a particularly hot day, Anna took a glass of water but, despite her thirst, pushed the glass away. For weeks she refused to drink until one day, while under hypnosis, she told Breuer how a dog had once drunk from a glass belonging to her governess, whom she disliked. After expressing anger and disgust at this memory, Anna freely drank water, awakening from hypnosis with the glass on her lips. The aversion ended once the symptom emerged with emotional intensity as it was being talked away. The cathartic method was said to work because "it brings an end to the operative force of the idea by allowing it to find a way out through speech."[17]

Their emphasis on strong emotions which characterize the initial trauma and must accompany catharsis inspired what is sometimes called Freud's economic model. Highly stressful situations typically elicit an energetic response—for example, a scream or flight—but if there is no catharsis and the emotion remains bottled up, the affect-laden idea persists in a sequestered state and a pathological condition ensues. Chronic symptoms are manifested when the patient reexperiences the pent-up emotions without being able to remember the concrete situation, the traumatic scene, in which they first occurred.

Breuer and Freud's analysis pictured the mind as a physiological system of forces comparable to the distribution of energy in an electrical circuit. According to Freud, the mind-nervous system naturally tends toward a constant (low) stage of psychic energy, or quantity of affect. Equilibrium, which he equated with health, is maintained by disposing of (abreacting) accumulated quantities of affect along pathways of normal, everyday mental and motor activity. But in hysteria, a certain quota is channeled or "converted" inappropriately into somatic symptoms. The aim of cathartic therapy was, from an economic point of view, to identify and discharge bottled-up affect along more normal, conscious pathways of mental and motor activity.

Medical and Symbolic Modes of Inquiry

The constancy principle led to Freud's theories about the regulating mechanism of the psyche, a fundamental assumption of psychoanalysis. Even so, the study of neuroses could not be easily contained by the concepts of physiology, physics, or biology. In De Anima, Aristotle referred to two methods for studying the emotions and illustrated how they differ by offering their corresponding definitions of anger. The dialectical method characterized anger as "the appetite for returning pain for pain," whereas the physical method would conceptualize the same phenomenon as "a boiling of blood or warm substance surrounding the heat."[18] Similarly, Freud engaged in two kinds of inquiry for investigating mental disorders: one relied upon the inherited discourse of his contemporaries, who treated the mind as if it were a physical network composed of discrete units, such as neurones, bearing a functional relationship to one another; the other employed the language of historical narrative, which inquires into how past episodes gather significance in the life of the patient. In the case of hysteria, neither method alone could encompass the disease in its entirety. One reveals the history of an individual's attempt to resolve conflict;

the other examines the neurological and physiological phenomena which instantiate general laws of behavior in the nervous system.

Freud would have confined the study of neuroses to physiology had his clinical work permitted it, but this form of explanation would have forced him to neglect the psychological implications of his observations. Granted the place of his "physical method" in the study of hysteria, the central message of the "Preliminary Communication" (1893) announced that "hysterics suffer from reminiscences," a maxim which cannot be understood except with reference to the patient's motives, his or her conflicting desires to both forget and conserve the past.[19] Freud observed that patients suffering from an abnormal attachment to the past were unduly troubled by traumatic events, dating as far back as childhood, which kept them from functioning normally in adult life. As a therapist, he sought to relieve the patient of the burden of the past, thereby enabling him or her to live more freely and fully in the present. But he also said that neurotics try to make the past nonexistent, a statement in seeming contradiction to his claim that neurotics remember only too well. Could it be that the neurotics do not remember well enough, that they pay dearly for forgetting decisive scenes from their remote past?

These two positions can be reconciled if we accept the idea that the past can be consciously forgotten while unconsciously remembered: if the neurotic "forgets" the past by suppressing it, he or she will be condemned to repeat old patterns of behavior and will manifest symptoms which reassert the traumatic scene in a cleverly disguised form. Whether we accent the first or second formulation, the cause and cure remain the same. The patient suffers from a failure of memory, which can be corrected only if he or she is assisted in coming to terms with the relevant past. Only by learning to remember, Freud implies, do people also learn to forget. We have touched upon two forms of memory in Freud's writing: representative memory, corresponding to the patient's labored recollections of past experiences as well as the analyst's technique for eliciting suppressed memories, and what I will provisionally call unconscious memories, the persistence of remote scenes which are expressed only indirectly and are inaccessible to conscious recall except under the extraordinary influence of the analyst. Remembering something ordinarily implies that one can locate the experience in the past and distinguish its representation from other states of affairs which currently exist. Freud included in this category preconscious memories—ideas temporarily forgotten or not present before the mind but always available to voluntary recall—as well as fully conscious recollection. Unconscious memories, however, are divorced from these modes of apprehending the past. Ordinarily, our memories pale and fade; especially painful memories are gradually weakened through repetition or associative connections which permit a linking of the distressful memory with other, more benign, memories and ideas. In the case of hysteria, however, the possibility of a normal defense through either attenuation or an associative network linking it to the rest of psychical life is unavailable to the patient. Instead the trauma which precipitates hysteria is so powerful, preserved with such striking clarity and freshness, that the neurotic's memories are not eradicated as he or she wishes but are imprisoned (eingeklemt) in what Charcot termed a condition seconde, intruding into the patient's conscious life in the guise of chronic symptoms.

The decisive shift in Freud's approach to the study of hysteria from his "physical" method to a "dialectical" one can be traced to his concern with the interpretation of memory symbols (Errinerungsymbol), a term he coined for symptoms which refer allusively to the history of the illness and particularly to the traumatic scene. In his Five Lectures on Psychoanalysis (1910), Freud compared the symptoms with monuments and memorials in order to show how neuroses are amenable to linguistic analysis as well as why hysterical reminiscences are distinctly pathological.[20] He cited the example of a pillar in London which stands to the memory of the great part of the city (lost by fire). A Londoner today who bemoaned the loss of the city, which long since has been rebuilt, would certainly be considered odd. The neurotic, Freud averred, behaves like the impractical Londoner, not merely in vividly recalling painful scenes from the distant past, but in being profoundly affected by them. A temporal incongruity or dislocation seems to have taken place, in which the scene has greater vivacity and significance in memory than in the proper context of its original occurrence.

Despite their similarities, neurotics differ from the Londoner in one important respect: they are blind to the historical significance or meaning of their symptoms, incapable of reading the past contained in their own memory symbols. A memory symbol which functions as a symptom actually involves two memories with no conscious link between them. One is the repressed memory of an unpleasant event; the other an apparently subordinate, concomitant memory. In the weak sense of symbolization, the latter refers to a circumstance contiguous in time or space to the traumatic event which cannot be brought to conscious memory. The significance and affect of the first unconscious memory is transferred to the second and conscious memory. Every new experience reminiscent of the trauma disturbs the unconscious memory, but it emerges in consciousness only as an intensification of the ostensibly benign, conscious memory. Stated differently, the individual becomes acutely aware not of the objectionable scene but of either a proximate event or the scene's opaque "memory symbol" (i.e., symptom). Hence, the compulsive ideas are apparently absurd until the work of analysis restores the dismembered symbol to its original connection with the traumatic scene. Freud offered the following explanation of symbol formation:

> Before the analysis, A is an excessively intense idea, which forces its way into consciousness too often, and each time gives rise to weeping. The subject does not know why he weeps at A; he regards it as absurd but cannot prevent it. After the analysis, it has been discovered that there is an idea B, which justifiably recurs frequently. . . . The affect of B is not absurd. It is intelligible to the subject. . . . B stands in a particular relation to A. For there has been an occurrence which consisted of B and A together. A was an incidental circumstance, B was appropriate for producing the lasting effect. The reproduction of this event in memory has now taken a form of such a kind that it is as though A had stepped into B's place. A has become a substitute, a symbol, for B.[21]

Normally one is aware of the relationship between the symbol and that which it symbolizes. To use Freud's example, a perfectly rational soldier may sacrifice his life for a piece of colored cloth on a pole, given his awareness of the nation that stands behind the symbol. Otherwise, we would find ourselves faced with the absurdity of a soldier capable of dying literally for a flag. In hysteria, however, B is repressed and the analysand does not know the connection between A and B.

A memory symbol in the strong sense referred to a more intimate connection between the symptom and repressed affect than association by contiguity to a trauma. A verbal phrase mediates conceputally—or thematically—between them. For example, the phrase "a slap in the face" can be repressed through the medium of the body and manifested in a facial neuralgia which concentrates affect in organic pain. Freud offered the following symbolic reconstruction of the symptom:

> When I began to call up the traumatic scene, the patient saw herself back in a period of great mental irritability towards her husband. She described a conversation which she had with him and a remark of his which she had felt as a bitter insult. Suddenly she put her hand to her cheek, gave a loud cry of pain and said: "It was like a slap in the face." With this her pain and her attack were both at an end.[22]

Symbolization involves the use of the body as a metaphor, a figure of speech: the "slap in the face" was inscribed, so to speak, in a facial neuralgia which displaces affect from psyche to soma.

In both weak and strong instances of symbolization, the neurotic forcibly bans from consciousness some painful truth about the past and achieves what Freud called a "proximate fulfillment of the task," that is, a compromise between the force of the pathogenic idea and the wish to forget it. Stated somewhat differently, the neurotic pays for his ignorance by having his own history haunt him in symptoms which obliquely symbolize the traumatic scene. Freud believed that bodily events and ideas perceived as symptomatic clues might reveal to the analyst precisely what the patient labored to conceal from himself. And once the repressed idea is recovered, the symptom is not merely explained but also resolved. The strategies of interpretation which aimed at finding the sense of the neurotic action, the link between the symptom and its motive or between the symbol and symbolized, moved Freud to explore territory which was foreign to, though not forbidden by, the economic point of view. Whatever the merits of a mechanics of conflict, psychoanalysis was emerging as a "semantics of desire" as well.[23]

How these two methods differ can be clarified by contrasting Freud and Breuer's views on the etiology of hysteria in their "Preliminary Communication." Both men agreed that hysteria is triggered by the patient's failure to respond adequately (i.e., emotionally or with sufficient affect) to a psychic trauma and that symptoms are resolved only when the therapist uncovers the events surrounding their initial appearance and elicits the patient's vivid recollection of the traumatic scene. They also concurred that hysteria exhibited a tendency toward dissociation of consciousness and somatic conversion of the distressful idea. However, they parted ways in explaining why a satisfactory reaction to a traumatic event does or does not occur in a given individual. Why, in other words, do some individuals but not others fall prey to "unconscious memories" and their attendant symptoms?

According to Breuer, dissociation of consciousness is due primarily to the patient's psychic state at the time of the trauma's occurrence: "We find among the causes of hysterical symptoms ideas which are not in themselves significant, but whose persistence is due to paralyzing affects, such as fright, and during positively abnormal psychic states."[24] Breuer's explanation, stated in terms of the accumulation of "mental energy" or "excitation of affect," accommodated the economic model of hysteria. It was particularly convincing in the case of Anna O., where nervous exhaustion due to caring for her father may have brought about an abnormal state which triggered her illness. The psychic-state hypothesis also supported Charcot's model for traumatic neurosis, where an accident induces a hypnotic state in which a relatively minor event, such as a mild blow to a limb, is capable of producing hysterical symptoms.

Freud acknowledged the existence of Breuer's "hypnoid

states" but believed that the nature of the traumatic event was primarily responsible for the genesis of hysteria. His clinical experience suggested that a specifically sexual experience which arouses an idea or impulse that is incompatible with the patient's moral beliefs might be sufficient to precipitate hysteria. Not surprisingly, Freud found that sufferers typically were continent women who had inhibited impulses toward what they viewed as aberrant or socially unacceptable behavior: "An occurrence of incompatibility took place in their ideational life—that is to say . . . their ego was faced with an experience, an idea or feeling, which induced such a distressing affect that the subject decided to forget about it because . . . [they] had no confidence in . . . [their] powers to resolve . . . [their] difficulties."[25]

Yet it was not clear to Freud at the time of his collaboration with Breuer why the hysteric's efforts at "counterwill" fail if people generally are successful in suppressing doubts and misgivings and in inhibiting impulses. Moreover, the sexual experiences which in Freud's cases appeared to be responsible for prompting repression often seemed quite innocuous and inadequate to elicit such responses, and it seemed to Freud as though predisposition must indeed play an essential role in the etiology of hysteria:

> In some cases, no doubt, we are concerned with experiences which must be regarded as severe traumas—rape perhaps. . . . But in other cases the experiences are astonishingly trivial. In one of my patients it turned out that her neurosis was based on the experience of a boy stroking her hand tenderly and, at another time, pressing his knee against her dress as they sat side by side at a table, while his expression let her see something forbidden. . . . If serious and trifling events alike . . . are to be recognized as the ultimate traumas of hysteria, then we may be tempted to hazard the explanation that hysterics are peculiarly constituted creatures—probably on account of some hereditary predisposition.[26]

Since it appeared that the content of ideas or emotions could not determine whether hysteria would ensue, Freud was not yet prepared to reject Breuer's psychic-state hypothesis. Nevertheless, he concentrated increasingly on those cases where the splitting of consciousness was not "spontaneous" or the direct result of fright or exhaustion but appeared to derive from an act of will on the part of the patient. He insisted that defense and the repression of inimical sexual memories traumatizing to the entire ego were the major factors in the etiological equation of hysteria. The illness simply could not be ascribed to the fortunes of genetic inheritance. The patient, Freud was convinced, did not merely fall ill but desired to be sick; that is, he or she would prefer harboring symptoms to consciously remembering morally repugnant events related to his or her sexual life.

Freud actually gave two versions of sexuality, one belonging to the defense model, inspired by his clinical experience of the patient's resistance to his efforts at identifying the source of neurotic symptoms, and the other restricted to the quasi-scientific study of somatic excitation as an energetic force that seeks discharge. The latter sense of the term applied to the study of neurasthenia and anxiety neuroses as strictly somatic complaints caused by the depletion or accumulation of excitation. Psychoanalysis, as it evolved from Freud's clinical studies of defense neuroses, centered on the distinctive values, wishes, and taboos associated with human sexual experience.[27]

The inadequacy of a strictly physiological conception for understanding psychic conflict and character is brought into relief by Breuer's own clinical experience in the treatment of Anna O. In his biography of Freud, Ernest Jones notes that Anna made sexual advances toward Breuer, which forced him to terminate therapy prematurely. Breuer, it might be argued, could tolerate behavior, however abnormal, provided that it carried the label of a symptom, but Anna's desire for him was intensely personal, an impropriety which abruptly placed their relationship outside a therapeutic context. Once Anna's character became inseparable from her disease, she challenged the rule of scientific neutrality which Breuer was obliged to enforce as a physician. Shocked by Anna's attempt to seduce him, Breuer subsequently shied away from clinical treatment and pursued theories which pictured the mind as an electrical current or machine whose parts sometimes fall into disequilibrium. Models such as these enabled him to conceptualize the disorder as an alien entity within the patient which could be isolated and observed without the patient's interference. As Philip Rieff points out, it was commonly believed that the "patient, like a feudal lady, was a spectator at the tournament for which he has engaged the physician as his champion, and the treatment— like the disease, once contracted—was something to which the patient could only submit."[28] It is true that Breuer had developed the talking cure, had engaged in verbal dialogue which was something more than an extraprofessional amenity. Nevertheless, once Anna refused to submit to his implicit demand that she play an essentially passive role in therapy, Breuer became startled and promptly called the game off.

Freud eventually interpreted the new twist in Anna's case much differently. Evidence that the neurosis involved substituting the therapist for, say, a parent who figured prominently in the traumatic scene indicated that the relationship between the therapist and neurotic was fundamentally unlike that between researcher and any other "object" of study. If, as Breuer had claimed, the patient must as a condition of cathartic therapy reenact the traumatic scene with its original intensity, then should transference not be played out as an essential part of the cure?

I wish to argue that the analogy of medical treatment for a physical disorder to therapy breaks down because it assumes that the problem can be resolved independently of the agency or intentions of the patient, albeit intentions curiously hidden by the patient from himself. This criticism of an exclusively mechanistic conception of mental disorders extends to the use of hypnosis as an instrument of therapy. Although it demonstrated the ideogenic character of hysteria, hypnosis shared one fatal flaw with hydrotherapy, electrotherapy, and other treatments which addressed hysteria as a blantantly physical, or nervous, disorder: they all treated the patient as the accidental host of the disease. Freud's enthusiasm for hypnosis was dampened by his clinical experience of the patient's symptoms abating only to reappear later. However, his chief objection was not that the method needed to be refined but that it ultimately obscured the purpose or motive of neurotic symptoms. "Hypnosis disguises, psychoanalysis reveals,"[29] Freud would later write in reviewing the development of his therapeutic technique.

We can appreciate Freud's point if we liken the use of hypnosis to an anesthetic which numbs the conscious, normal self in order to gain access to pathological material. By inducing a hypnotic state, the physician can elicit ideas and emotions belonging to a sequestered psychic state. Once the pathogenic memories have been extirpated, the physician awakens the patient, who presumably is now in an improved state of mental health. Let us assume that, as in the case of Elizabeth von R., the patient protests, "I'm not asleep you know; I can't be hypnotized."[30] We might say that both Anna O. and Elizabeth von R., because they refused to be subdued, were poor candidates for treatment. If the patient will not cooperate, resists suggestions by the analyst, or disregards protocol, the analyst can no longer observe the rules which effectively separate the analyst from the patient and the patient from her disease.

Psychoanalysis properly begins with Freud's recognition that hysteria cannot be circumscribed by the physical methods of anatomy or physiology, since they cannot comprehend human motivation or the linguistic character of ideas embodied in physical symptoms. Breuer's hypnotic technique ultimately obscured persistent emotional conflict by construing the patient's resistance to his commands as an obstacle to the study and treatment of hysteria. Freud learned that conflict between the analysand and the analyst, as well as within the patient, elucidates the patient's motives for suppressing or distorting past experiences, for confounding the therapist or deliberately impeding treatment, for prolonging symptoms in spite of the expressed desire to be cured. The economic point of view proved inadequate, since it could not address the intersubjective drama of emotional conflict, whether staged in the family romance or the therapy hour. Adhering to Charcot's teaching that clinical observations should take precedence over theoretical considerations, Freud turned increasingly to the diverse life stories of his patients—to the interpretation of their memory symbols—for an understanding of the origin of hysteria and a new key to the study of humankind.

2

Psychoanalysis as Narrative

Trained in medicine and physiology, Freud endeavored to bring the rigor and certitude of these disciplines to his study of neuroses, dreams, and the basic features of mental life. However, his tools of analysis, as Freud himself ruefully admitted, more closely resembled the artifice of the storyteller than the careful testing of hypotheses by a technician in his laboratory.

> I was not always a psychotherapist, but was trained in local electrical diagnosis like other neuro-pathologists, and I find it a very strange thing that case histories I describe still read like short stories and lack, so to speak, the serious imprint of science. I must console myself with the thought that it is obviously the nature of the material itself that is responsible for my own choice. In the study of hysteria logical diagnosis and electric reactions do not come into the picture, while an exhaustive account of mental processes, of the kind we are accustomed to, enables me, by the application of a few psychological laws, to obtain a kind of insight into the origins of hysteria.[1]

Having discovered that mental disorders cannot be adequately explained as organic disturbances, Freud located their origin and genesis in the individual's personal history. Clinical study and treatment now required scrutiny of unrepeatable scenes from the patient's past in order to uncover the meaning of current symptoms. The conceptual analysis of narrative that follows rests on a threefold distinction: the "events" that precipitate and organize the patient's illness, as what happened (Freud's "material itself") in the patient's distant past; the patient's incomplete and disjointed report of what happened during the therapy hour; and the analyst's effort to edit the patient's report to make its purpose clear, that is, to instill the report with intelligibility and thereby make it accessible to the patient.

The interplay of the features of narrative in the case history introduces a basic tension in psychoanalytic explanation: first, between "what happened" and the analysand's editorial revisions and, second, between the analysand's report and the analyst's editorial revisions. Knowledge of "what happened" in the historical past cannot be equated with the direct inspection of discrete events investigated by empirical science. Any penetration into the past implies an interpretive act in which the "facts" are themselves shaped by the interests—I should say desires—and language guiding the analyst's inquiry as well as the analysand's resistances. The case of facial neuralgia symbolizing a "slap in the face" illustrates how the nucleus of a neurotic illness is inseparable from the patient's system of beliefs and linguistic associations.

The analyst shares with the historian the necessity of reconstructing the past from textual evidence. Although the historian may have direct access to agents who have participated in recent events, he or she works primarily with documents. Once the documents have been retrieved and deciphered, the historian's task remains to determine why the author selected a particular set of events as significant and whether the author's bias or limited point of view led him or her to distort the historical record. The historian then evaluates competing or alternative accounts of the same episode to reach a judgment about each document's authenticity, completeness, and accuracy.

Interpretive choices in both history and psychoanalysis are necessitated by the simultaneous richness and sparseness of the historical record. The wealth of available material documenting a particular region of the past could not possibly be represented in a single, coherent account. The analyst and historian both must judge which incidents shall count as facts and, conversely, which should be discounted as peripheral details that could only obscure their purpose or untrack their story line. Because the past does not always leave a trace and so eludes the historical record (or the analysand's report), the analyst and historian also face the common task of supplying missing connections through acts of interpretive reconstruction.

Recent debate about the explanatory requirements of historical inquiry tends to oppose narrative and analytical forms of explanation.[2] Historians and philosophers who favor the analytical form of explanation argue that the study of the human past is no different from any other science which tests lawlike hypotheses about a specific kind of behavior. In this view, even widely disparate episodes can instantiate the same laws—require the same explanation—if they share similar antecedents. This form of explanation offers the advantage of generalization and abstraction. An ostensibly rival form of explanation, narrative reconstruction places emphasis on the patterning or plotting of a genetic sequence as a distinctive temporal configuration.

Without prejudging the value of the analytical form of explanation, which will be considered shortly, I do want to suggest that narrative explanation is indispensable for understanding the historical past, including the history of the analysand, and more generally for assessing the aims and methods of psychoanalysis. Narrative explanation relies on hindsight because its function is to discern what happened *after* the event has occurred. Although the historian may err by uncritically projecting contemporary standards or assumptions upon earlier periods, the unavoidable gap between the historian's understanding of the past and the self-understanding of historical agents need not imply the problem of relativism. As Arthur Danto has observed, the goal of the historian is not to simulate an eyewitness account: "The whole point of history is not to know actions as witnesses might, but as historians do—in connection with later events as parts of a temporal whole."[3] An incident is explained when the temporal process of which it is a part exhibits an intelligible structure.

The material of the historian is ultimately human action ar-

rayed as a genetic relationship of antecedents and consequences, where the latter emerge from and internalize the former. Because a historical event is temporally complex and
because the purpose of inquiry is not prediction but retrodic-
tion, it would be inappropriate to characterize history as a
methodological cousin of either natural science or social sciences which emulate its methods. The objection might be
raised that I have defined history too narrowly by excluding
such sciences as geology and astronomy, which examine non-
human phenomena under conditions of historical change. Although we may speak loosely about the application of general
laws to the "history" of, say, the Mississippi River, this manner
of contrasting historical method and its object-domain is misleading because the actions of historians and historical agents
alike are intentionally complex events which incorporate references to their own past. If human events combine to make history, and humans make sense of their world by interpreting
their past, history necessarily consists in the (historian's) *interpretations of* (historical agents') *interpretations*. Frederick
Olafson explains this peculiarity of historical inquiry in the
"semantic complexity" common to the perspective of the historian, the historical agent, and the reader who follows the narrative account. In his own words, "This [perspective] deviates
from a conception of the relationship in which thought and inquiry stand to their object in natural science. Their objects do
not, as it were, 'talk back.' "[4]

This characterization of history certainly applies to the work
of psychoanalysis. Despite their asymmetry, affinities between
the historian (analyst) and historical agent (analysand) are implicit in the historicity that they both share; for, again, both
have the capacity to situate themselves in a temporal sequence
through the reconstruction of events in their own past. If, as I
wish to claim, the principal focus of psychoanalysis is the case
study, then what merits being called a historical fact must be
situated in the therapeutic dialogue and its written exposition.
As Paul Ricoeur has observed, the wishes and desires of the
analysand become an "object" for the analyst only when he is
forced to speak. "This screening through speech in the analytic

situation functions as a criterion for what will be held to be the object of this science: not instinct as physiological phenomenon, not even desire as energy, but desire as a meaning capable of being deciphered, translated, and interpreted."[5] The facts of psychoanalysis, continues Ricoeur, are themselves *reports* which belong to the historical record. We know dreams only upon awakening, and symptoms become intelligible only in relation to other incidents or associations communicated in the report. Desire becomes a datum of psychoanalysis when inscribed in narrative, recounted in stories which do not so much reproduce as structure the life of the analysand. The mental constructions of the analysand are symbolized expressions which demand interpretation.

Adolf Grünbaum has accused Ricoeur of distorting and truncating psychoanalytic theory by limiting its subject matter to verbal exchanges between the analyst and the analysand.[6] In his view, Ricoeur errs by attributing language or symbolism not merely to representations of psychic phenomena but to the phenomena themselves. The dream, for example, attests to the work of unconscious repression and instinctual forces even if we do gain access to its mechanisms through the analysand's report of its manifest content. Psychoanalysis, he continues, should not be considered immune from the requirement of testability simply because its phenomena are known only indirectly through the medium of language. How does Freud differ, Grünbaum queries, from the physicist who can observe subatomic particles only as tracks in a Wilson cloud chamber. If we neither discount the physicist's experiments nor claim that they depart from the procedures of normal science, then why should psychoanalysis be treated as a special case?

As mentioned, what distinguishes psychoanalytic inquiry from, say, physics is that past events—"what happened"— share the same ontological status as the mode of inquiry which apprehends the past: the subject matter of history cannot be sharply demarcated from its verbal representation. Narrative, in other words, is not simply a medium for inquiry into empirical events but, in Barbara Hardy's words, "a primary act of the mind," a structure inherent in human experience and action.[7] As a consequence, it makes sense to cast the relationship between "method" and "object" as a kind of dialogue. Seen in this light, psychoanalysis cannot be understood in the same terms as subatomic physics. Rather than examining how the accuracy of Freud's explanations can be tested, we should ask what *authorizes* a particular story, whether supplied by the analyst, the analysand, or the exchange between them.

If psychoanalysis cannot claim the kind of certitude associated with empirical science, its scientific status still depends on the accurate depiction of the patient's past in relating the etiology of the illness and in bringing about a cure. Otherwise, Kraft-Ebing, one of Freud's teachers, would have good reason for accusing Freud of telling "scientific fairy tales." The question of whether psychoanalysis should be considered a science actually addresses two philosophical issues: the empirical problem of validation and the logical problem regarding the explanatory features of psychoanalysis as a putative science. As I argue in the second section of this chapter, psychoanalysis does possess the logical features of scientific explanation. The explanatory context of the case history is a response to some incongruity in the analysand's behavior, a puzzle taking one of two forms: an inconsistency, where one piece of knowledge is incompatible with previous observations or beliefs, or an undetected coherence, where one piece of information bears no apparent relationship to the body of knowledge about the analysand.[8] The demand for explanation arises from an inability to fit either conflicting or disparate phenomena into some organized and comprehensible whole. During the therapy hour, the analyst must draw out the story implicit in the events recounted by the patient. Together analyst and analysand probe the significance—in Freud's terms, the "latent content"—dwelling beneath the surface of the patient's overt behavior and speech.

The problem of validation arises because the editing necessary to make the analysand's report comprehensible risks doing violence to the only direct source of evidence—the only "literal history"—available to the analyst. The patient's verbal report, itself symptomatic of his or her illness, suffers from narrative insufficiency due to distortion or (partial) amnesia; that is, it lacks the intelligibility needed to provide a compelling genetic explanation. If the patient's report is not trustworthy as an account of his or her life history, how can the analyst be certain that his or her editorial revisions have not imposed, by means of manipulation or suggestion, a distorted picture of the illness, which nevertheless wins the analysand's acceptance? The analyst's finished narrative conceivably has therapeutic efficacy but lacks the accuracy required for it to have explanatory value. To restate the problem in Kantian terms, dramatic unity without fidelity to the stubborn facts is blind, whereas a chronicle without narrative binding is conceptually empty. The case history must steer a middle course between the fictional unities of imaginative literature and the demands of empirical science in the study of human motivation and action.

Story and History

The narrative organization of events in Freud's case histories all contain several stories, including the narration of a segment of the patient's life, of the duration of illness, and of the investigation and treatment of the illness. Precisely what do we mean by storytelling and how is it wedded to historical inquiry?

The earliest and perhaps the most authoritative discussion of this question appears in Aristotle's *Poetics*. According to Aristotle, merely successive events must be integrated into a plot which has a distinct beginning, middle, and end; and the scope of a dramatic narrative must coincide with the unity of the action it seeks to convey: "The truth is that, just as in other imitative acts, one imitation is always of one thing, so in poetry the story, as an imitation of action, must represent one action, a complete whole, with its several incidents so closely connected that the transposal or withdrawal of one will disjoin and dislocate the whole."9 If we extend this characterization of poetry to the study of history, then a historical event should receive its definition from its contribution to the development of a plot. Reciprocally, a plot emerges as a way of connecting event and story. As Ricoeur writes, "A story is *made out of* events to the extent that plot *makes events into* a story."[10]

The case of Elizabeth von R., Freud's first extensive published case history, offers a good example of storytelling for assessing the place of narration in psychoanalysis.[11] Indeed, Freud's own reflections on the status of storytelling, quoted earlier, appear in the discussion immediately following his summary of Elizabeth's illness. Freud meets Aristotle's requirement of narrative coherence when he describes Elizabeth's illness as a story of emotional conflict consisting of three episodes: the emergence of conflict between filial piety and erotic desire; emotional pain and acute physical distress resulting from her failure to reconcile her sexual desires with her moral beliefs; and the resolution of conflict and alleviation of suffering through the ministrations of the analyst.

In Elizabeth's case, the protagonist is an individual with moral purpose and basically good character who falls from happiness to misery because of either a moral flaw or a profound error in judgment. Typically, tragedies also involve a change in the hero's fortunes from ignorance to knowledge, as in *Oedipus*, where the messenger, coming to gladden Oedipus and to remove his fears regarding his mother, reveals the shocking secret of his birth. Similarly, Elizabeth is a virtuous young woman—fiercely independent, sensitive, and utterly devoted to her family—who, because of a regrettable act of will, denies her erotic feelings toward a family friend and also toward her brother-in-law. Her symptoms are, in Rieff's words, "dubiously useful errors with which a sufferer hides some truth from himself."[12] Freud reveals that Elizabeth, even as she suffered, never suspected why she experienced pains in her legs. Her self-deception made her blind to the significance of her physical symptoms, which symbolized the principal scenes of conflict and, therefore, the source of her unhappiness. At this point, Freud's case history veers sharply from the course marked by Aristotle. Although Freud insisted in his later writings that analysis can only transform hysterical misery into common unhappiness, he nonetheless insisted in his case histories that the moment of self-discovery greatly improves the patient's prospects for happiness, a turn which finds no parallel in Greek tragedy. As a clinician Freud was convinced that the termination of therapy is announced by the dissolution of symptoms as the patient gains freedom from the burden of incidents properly belonging to his or her distant past.

Can we conclude that Aristotle's description of the narrative structure of a poetic work approximates the organization of narrative material in writing history? Aristotle did not think so, denigrating the work of the historian for describing merely what happened rather than what is "probable or necessary." The distinction, he wrote, "consists in this, . . . that one describes the thing that has been, and the other a kind of thing that might be. Hence poetry is something more philosophical and of a graver import than history, since its statements are of the nature of universals, whereas those of history are singular."[13]

Aristotle did not object specifically to the practice of historians such as Herodotus who put their observations into verse. He did insist that despite the appearance of order in historical writing, the study of contingent times and places in the past is epistemologically inferior to dramatic works which express essential truths admitting of neither time nor diversity. Both poetry and history traffic in specific incidents, but poetry magnifies and dramatizes particular episodes to convey essential, recurring truths about the human condition. History, by contrast, is constrained by its obligation to verisimilitude, the faithful representation of particular events as they actually happened. Because the particular events of poetry dramatize universal truths, invented episodes arguably possess greater veracity than the contingent, accidental attributes rendered by the historian.

Although we have entered the realm of fiction to elaborate the methods of historical inquiry, we now find, ironically, that poetic work provides a model of philosophic—that is, universal and necessary—truths superior to the presumably objective, "scientific" histories of Freud. Poesis, or making, today connotes "fiction," but Aristotle never regarded invention as an enemy to truth seeking. Poetic works exhibit what Aristotle termed "internal necessity," that is, a necessary connection among events which proceed from a natural beginning to a natural end. The incidents chronicled by historians, by contrast, are not purposive, directed toward a *telos*. History, devoid of plot, is poetry's epistemological inferior.

Christian philosophers who contested Aristotle's position sought to illumine the progression of history as a clue to the design and direction imposed upon it by God's will. Consequently, history in the Middle Ages was not regarded as an arbitrary succession, a meaningless concatenation of events, but as an intelligible process guided by the immanent law or transcendent design (i.e., masterplot) of a divine intelligence (i.e., author). God's authority in the unfolding drama of human events may have been shaken by the rise of science, but the proximity of history and literature, particularly in its epic form, persisted well into the eighteenth century. "My aim," declared Voltaire,

> has been to make a great picture of events that are worthy of being painted, and to keep the reader's eye trained on the leading character. History, like tragedy, requires an exposition, a central action, a denouement. . . . I hate petty facts. . . . My secret is to free the reader to wonder: Will Phillip V ascend to the throne? . . . In short, I have tried to move my reader, even in history.[14]

The philosophes accepted Aristotle's characterization of poetry but not his claim for its specific difference from history. Hugh Blair, an eighteenth-century rhetorician, perhaps came closest to claiming for the historian the task Aristotle had reserved for the poets: "In the conduct and management of his subject, the possible requisite in an historian is to give as much unity as possible; that is, his history should not consist of separate unconnected parts merely, but should be bound together by some connecting principle, which shall make the impression on the mind of something that is one, whole, and entire."[15]

This rhetorical or literary preoccupation with the effects of historical writing on the attentive reader has yielded in our time to the primacy of epistemological concerns, to notions of objectivity, evidence, and method. Contemporary historians enforce Aristotle's separation of their discipline from poetry; but now they reverse the unequal relationship by celebrating the actual and disdaining invention as an impediment to knowledge. This is not to say that historians and philosophers have not been alive to the contribution of the observer to what counts as historical fact. Nevertheless, historians respect the need for evidence and place this requirement before the need to discern form or unity in their material. The association of imagination with poetry, coupled with growing skepticism concerning the reality of universals except as the logical form of natural laws, has generally led to the devaluation of fiction by philosophers as a source of knowledge. The study of history, in turn, remains a second-order truth but now in the service of empirical science rather than imaginative literature.[16]

A significant dissenting position on this issue, one that both Aristotle and the quanto-historians would find offensive, boldly asserts that history is saturated with fiction, that is, with figural language or tropes—metaphor, metonymy, synechdoche, and irony—that exploit the full range of fictional discourse. Against the normative separation of history and literature on epistemological grounds, Hayden White has identified tropes and distinctive narrative patterns—"modes of emplotment"—as the culturally endowed conditions of historical consciousness.[17] Jacques Lacan and recent literary critics influenced by his writings have explicitly transposed Freud's terminology of energetics into the language of tropes by grounding the activity of signification in the unconscious operations of the psyche. Displacement, for example, is recast as metonymy and condensation as metaphor in such manifestations of desire as dreams and symptoms.[18]

Freud's expressed attitude toward fictional narrative was ambivalent. He feared that his cases would be dismissed as mere short stories, but he also expressed admiration and envy of writers—notably Goethe, Sophocles, Shakespeare, and Schiller—for their capacity to grasp truths that the psychologist wins only by slow work. Literature, he conceded, intuitively anticipates the same truths which science will eventually recognize and methodically demonstrate: "Storytellers are valuable allies, and their testimony is to be rated high, for they usually know many things between heaven and earth that are not yet dreamt of in our philosophy. In psychological insights, indeed, they are not far ahead of people, because they draw on sources that have not yet been made accessible to science."[19] But after granting priority of insight to literature, Freud cautioned that only the methods and criteria of the sciences can separate the kernel of truth from the husk of illusion. The test of historical accuracy, as the *Poetics* remind us, does not enter into the composition or interpretation of literature. By contrast with history, humans who are portrayed in literature need not exist outside the bounds of the text, and their actions are controlled by an author whose powers are stymied in the real, contingent world. Consequently, Freud was compelled to invoke the authority of science as the sole arbiter of intuitions found in imaginative literature.

I think a stronger relationship between fiction and historical narrative can be detected in Freud's case studies. Literature arguably offers a better model of historical inquiry than natural science because it exemplifies how people change in response to acknowledged or avoided episodes from their significant past. Literature also brings into relief how the past may be retrieved or appropriated through the interpretations that agents, as well as others who know them, place upon their actions. This commitment to storytelling in historical inquiry as well as fictional narrative is rooted in a basic human need—the desire for sense. It is natural—or perhaps second nature—to humanize perceptions of merely successive events by endowing them with significance. Even the interval between "tick" and "tock," observes Frank Kermode, is charged with significant duration: " 'Tick' is a humble genesis, 'tock' a feeble apocalypse." "The interval," he continues, "must be purged of simple chronicity, of the emptiness of tock-tick, humanly uninteresting successiveness."[20]

The movement from *chronos* (a sequence of identical instants) to *kairos* (a time of reckoning and transformation in history) marks the transition from the study of physical motion in Newtonian science to the study of human action in psychoanalysis. The intentional life of the analysand, and the manner in which he or she confers organization and form on his or her life, invites the narrative structure elaborated by the analyst. Every historical agent—whether analyst or analysand—is poised between the horizons of beginning and ending and tries to achieve temporal integration of his or her memories, perceptions, and expectations. The plotting required to integrate "tick" and "tock" offers a primitive example of how people organize time—beginnings and endings—in their desire to make sense of themselves and their world. The plotting by which consciousness extends itself always presupposes an end (*telos*) that confers duration and meaning upon the whole. Hence, storytelling cannot be dismissed as fiction or patronized as a precursor to scientific truths which substitute laws for tales. Quite the opposite, the plotting and temporal integration constitutive of stories is indispensable for both the exercise of psychoanalytic interpretation and Freud's vision of humans as symbolizing—that is, sense-making and sense-disguising—animals.

Turning Story into History

The teleological ordering required for expression of self-understanding in historical agents was reaffirmed in Freud's psychoanalytic narratives. It remains to be seen how psychoanalysis converts the patient's story into history; for the historian (analyst) can justify his or her narrative only in light of the quite different story of how it was constructed. When do we accept the analysand's testimony and when do we challenge it? What ground rules, if any, guide the analyst's transformation of the analysand's story into the finished narrative account of his or her childhood and current illness? What evidence can be gathered to demonstrate that the analyst's account is superior to the analysand's autobiographical remarks? Finally, how can the analyst discern errors in his or her own judgment?

Freud vaguely sensed that his case histories might be too well formed. Was it possible that he prized the unity of a "fictional" plot over fidelity to the contingencies of historical events? Unlike authors who possess the creative license to arrange incidents to further their dramatic purposes, analysts/editors have neither the freedom nor the obligation to snip loose ends that might violate Aristotle's thematic unities of plot and character. Again, history claims to be descriptive and must verify its assertions, even if doing so jeopardizes the drama recommended by Voltaire or the coherence and unity desired by Hugh Blair.

The distinction between what happened as reported by a historical agent and the historian's reconstructed story of the past can be more sharply drawn by rehearsing Haskell Fain's discussion of "The Tale of Many Tongues."[21] Let us say that a sheet of paper is circulated among several people who are sitting at a table. Each person writes a single sentence which moves along the composition of the story. In order to write the story, each contributor would have to assume that he or she were carrying out the original intention of an author, even though authorial intention obviously is irreducible to the project of any single contributor. The historian might be likened to an editor who modifies the text to make its story more intelligible while preserving as much as possible of the original version. Editorial clarification can be readily justified once the historian identifies a transcendent purpose or authorial intention that controls the development of the entire story. By bringing this intention into relief, the historian can show what actually happened, the story previously hidden from view. The presumption of a coherent story line or theme guides the historian's editorial work, but if the ideas under consideration do not belong to a narrative scheme, as in "The Tale of Many Tongues," then the drive toward coherence may produce a fiction which falsifies an essentially *random* collection of sentences. As the piece of paper is passed from one person to the next, the sentences accumulate but they don't "add up." The writing deciphered by the historian/narrator may have no narrative line of development, no internal necessity which joins the various "episodes" in a well-integrated plot. Instead, we are left with a list of unrelated sentences, each explained by reference to the private thoughts of a particular author.

The lesson of Fain's "tale" is twofold. First, if the past consists of a multiplicity of stories which do not cohere, the historian/editor misrepresents his or her subject by stitching them together in the fabric of a narrative, a unified pattern threaded by a singular purpose or intention. Yet, and this is the second lesson, individual historical agents may not appreciate the significance—or insignificance—of their actions in light of some larger developing story. Fain explains:

> Suppose the historian/editor submits his improved version of the tale to the scrutiny of its authors, and some of them complain that certain of the lines they contributed were altered beyond recognition or omitted altogether. "But don't you see," the editor will retort, "some of the lines you wrote were not integrated into the story, were ignored by the other players, and were in fact so many lost opportunities." Should the historian deal with might-have-beens or with what actually happened?[22]

Just as the syntax of the sentences mislead us into assuming the dramatic unity of a "tale," the coherence of a plot may tempt us to impose a fraudulent outline on fortuitous events. Yet it is not clear that conscious reasons always indicate why something happened. The historian's reconstruction of the past may be suggested by the "logic of the whole story," the end of which is not yet in sight for those who are making it. For example, a diligent historian who read the tale would not confine his or her inquiry to its internal structure or development. Like any document or written record, the tale would be placed in a larger retrospective context for clues regarding the circumstances of its composition. The historian might discover, say, that the tale was an experiment in sentence combining or a game designed to trick any unsuspecting historian who later ventured to interpret it. The historian's version still differs from the intentions of the individual contributors, but the selection of a plausible principle of development now justifies his or her decision to omit some lines or not to integrate others into the story.

Although a speculative history which ignores individual intentions risks misrepresentation, it is not clear that conscious reasons always indicate why something happened. To take an-

other example drawn from Fain's text, the historical significance of Hitler's decision to invade Russia could not be discerned by inspecting Hitler's motive, that is, by examining the
situation as he envisioned it. Instead, the decision would have
to be described with reference to a story hidden from Hitler,
namely the demise of Germany in World War II. We can still
maintain that historical inquiry concerns the understanding of
why X did Y. However, we now see that Hitler—like con-
querors before him—badly miscalculated the effects of his decision. To tell this story of Hitler's folly, we appeal not to the
agent's conscious reasons but to the *incongruity* between his
intentions and their unforeseen consequences.

In both examples, Fain does not finally urge the reader to
abandon the teleological mode of explanation. It would be
more accurate to say that he recognizes the need to employ simultaneously two modes of explanation: the comprehension of
events as the striving of an agent to fulfill a goal and the observation of causally connected events or states.[23] These two
modes of explanation do not oppose one another but represent
the dual perspective that characterizes historical discourse. If
we examine the past from a retrospective point of view, nar-
rated events appear causally determined. The prospective point
of view tries to envision the expectations and intentions of the
agent or agents who participate in events as they unfold. The
first perspective enables us to see the condition under which
the "tale" was produced. The second enables us to understand
the intention which united the actions of all who contributed
to the tale's composition. Although these points of view are
complementary, they also permit us to distinguish between story and history (i.e., the story of the tale's composition).

This line of reasoning accords with W. B. Gallie's narrativist
view of the historical process as analogous to a game.[24] As
spectators we cannot predict with certainty the game's outcome, yet we intently follow the action with the assurance that
its promised resolution will be *retrospectively* comprehensible.
In both cases, surprises and contingencies maintain suspense,
but by unpacking the elements of the game/history in light of its
resolution, we can detect a coherence or unity of events that
could not be appreciated during their original development.

Freud believed that as editor/analyst he could not ignore the intentions and motives of the individual whose story he was telling. However, his solution was ultimately Hegelian in the sense that the analyst, like the philosopher of history, is granted privileged access to the subject's past, which enables him or her to discern in *rebus gestis* a logic of significance, or "cunning of reason," that eludes the agent whose past is being interrogated. The incompleteness, vagueness, or incoherence of the patient's report does not indicate the absence of order or plot but its double meaning as both an underlying unity and a deliberate ruse or scheme to conceal something of significance.

> Thus almost everywhere noticeable gaps, disturbing repetitions and obvious contradictions have come about—indications which reveal things to us which it was not intended to communicate. In its implications the distortion of a text resembles a murder: the difficulty is not in penetrating the deed, but in getting rid of its traces. We might well lend the word *Enstellung* to the double meaning to which it today makes no use. It should mean not only "to change the appearance of something" but also to "put something in another place, to displace." Accordingly, in many instances of textual distortion, we may nevertheless count upon finding what has been suppressed and disavowed, hidden somewhere else, though changed and torn from its context. Only it will not always be easy to recognize it.[25]

Fain's tale was a text that appeared to express the intention of purpose of a single author. Apparent unity, however, disguised the underlying absence of unity, the private thoughts of several "authors" without a shared intention among them. The psychic text of the illness or dream generally lacks the appearance of order or coherence; yet this fact only strengthened Freud's belief that the author's artifice was responsible for the dislocations that betrayed an original context of meaning. The analyst, too, "translates" the meaning of the work to those who are not yet fully aware of its true significance. Freud resembled Sherlock Holmes in his confidence that methodical inquiry could demonstrate how all human action is motivated and comprehensible to the perceptive observer. By applying the psychoanalytic method to symptomatic clues, he would eventually discover a moment of trauma, the scene of the crime which illuminates the meaning and significance of subsequent events in the case.

The analyst's story of the illness and the patient's report are both tied to the idea of defense understood as the scene of intrapsychic conflict that dramatizes the patient's history and as the strategy by which the patient tries "to get rid of the murder's traces," to conceal the meaning of his or her actions from the analyst. These two functions of defense converge in the interpretation of symptoms during the therapy hour. Freud discovered that when he elicited a painful memory from the patient, the symptoms would persist as long as the patient was under the influence of the objectionable idea. The symptoms would reach a climax when the patient was in the act of telling Freud the essential and decisive part of what he or she had to communicate, and with the last word the pain would disappear. In this way the pains would serve as an index of the thoroughness of the investigation and the significance of the issues raised by the analyst. Freud suspected that the symptoms served the purpose of defending against the analyst's forays into past incidents which the patient was determined to forget. The patient's motive for concealing an "incompatible idea" was interpreted as a sure sign the analyst was on the right track and should persist, in the manner of a prosecuting attorney, in the questioning; for the intensity of the patient's resistance was thought to be proportionate to its importance in the explanation of the illness.

By comprehending and countering the patient's tactics to keep him at bay during the therapy hour, Freud came to appreciate how and why these same strategies were employed by patients much earlier in life to keep their innermost desires hidden from themselves. Here, again, we see the interplay between the patient's report and the story of the analyst. The set of events initially recounted by Freud would say something about the patient's past but would offer few clues regarding the origin and development of the illness. In the case of Elizabeth, for example, Freud found that "it was a case history made up of commonplace emotional upheaval and there was nothing about it to explain why it was particularly from hysteria that she fell ill or why her hysteria took the particular form of abasia."[26] It remained to be seen how the event of Elizabeth's adolescence functioned as elements of a familiar kind of configuration. The story line, or plot, entered the scene of the therapy hour from the side of the patient's symptomatology. The bodily symptoms represented the intersection of the past (the symbol of painful events and impulses from childhood) and present (the scene of their reenactment in the therapy hour). Although Freud often referred to symptoms as a mechanism for the purpose of defense, it would be more accurate to say that the conflict symbolized by the symptom represents a kind of plot, again understood as both the embodiment of a scene which organizes the patient's life and a scheme in which the patient's wishes or desires are actively avoided or disavowed. Freud believed that by deciphering symptoms, the patient could be made privy to the story of his or her own life, and once the circumstances surrounding the patient's illness were placed in a narrative sequence organized around the theme of defense, the symptoms associatively tied to those events could be mastered and replaced by conscious memories and public, living language.

I have noted that the human tendency to imbue events with significance does not imply that one story is as good as another—the possibility of error or (self) deception is present in the stories we tell about ourselves and others. The analyst justifies his redescription of the patient's own account by postulating unconscious or latent reasons the patient might have for disavowing any knowledge of an incident or vigorously denying the truth of editorial revisions which seek to improve the intelligibility of the analysand's past.

Accuracy and Efficacy in Editing

How does the analyst interpret and modify the analysand's story to recover the truth about the analysand's past? Freud maintained as a "fundamental rule" of psychoanalytic technique that the analysand should spontaneously express his or her thoughts. The analyst, in turn, should maintain an attitude of "freely suspended attention" to avoid premature judgments that might halt or inhibit the analysand's unedited report. Attuned to the analysand's seemingly random remarks, the analyst can "catch the drift of the patient's unconscious with his own unconscious."[27] Freud likened this complementary relationship to a traveler who describes the passing landscape to an interested companion as he peers outside the carriage window.[28]

As Donald Spence points out, once we identify the analysand as the' author of his or her story and the analyst as its editor/reader, the question arises whether either party can obey the fundamental rule. If the analysand presents an incoherent—but truthful—stream of associations, then the analyst must "read" the cryptic text at the risk of imposing his or her own prejudices upon the analysand's story. If, instead, the analyst is presented with a lucid, comprehensible account, then we may ask whether the analysand has not violated the fundamental rule by editing his or her thoughts in the wish to satisfy the analyst's expectations.

Spence argues that unwitting interpretations emanating from analyst and analysand alike jeopardize the claims of psychoanalysis to the status of historical truth.[29] Case studies, he believes, should be regarded instead as "artistic creations" that impart order and unity to the patient's (fictionalized) life story. This line of reasoning fails to address Freud's radical claim that analysands cannot help but betray their past through their present actions and speech. As Janet Malcolm notes, "The analyst does not rely on the story that the patient tries to tell but the story he tells in spite of himself."[30] This story behind the story, as she calls it, must be inferred from the patient's behavior toward the analyst (transference) and from his or her manner of disobeying the fundamental rule of free association (resistance). Freud insisted that the analysand's silences, hesitations, and evasive gestures should be construed as signs of resistance which point to significant untold elements of the patient's story. Whether in word or deed, the analysand unwittingly repeats archaic patterns of belief which reveal enduring historical truths.

Freud's critics also have argued that the justification of his stories rested on a dubious notion of the unconscious as a compartment within the mind which denies access to the "I" while housing all thoughts and motives that have been banned from consciousness.[31] The image of the unconscious as a black box or shadow reality discounts the analysand's understanding of his or her own desires, thereby setting up a sharp contrast between appearances (manifest content; verbal report) and reality (the analyst's reconstructed story). The analyst's edited version is, in this reading, the discovery of an active but hidden reality. The belief that unconscious motives really existed in the past and operate with a vengeance in the present suggests a variation of the Cartesian ghost in the machine, an invisible duplicate of the events and motives normally identified with conscious mental life. For example, when he spoke of "interpolating" another link in the chain of consciously remembered events, Freud implied that the hidden link is of the same kind as known events. Dream thoughts also are treated as preformed, so that when they are uncovered in the process of analysis, the analyst matches his interpretation with the significant text residing beneath the manifest content. Given the analogy of the palimpsest, we might say that knowledge of the psyche's latent content is won by lifting the overlay of manifest content to display the integrity of the original, underlying text.

Joan Reeves has observed that Freud's treatment of the unconscious was colored by his tendency to treat all thinking according to the analogy of vision, as a process which integrates the "contents" of the mind.[32] A more plausible interpretation at first glance, one which does not image the mind as a suite of rooms, turns on the distinction between having an intention and the ability or willingness to articulate it.[33] Instead of endorsing Freud's early topography, which divides conscious and unconscious mental life into separate regions of the mind (i.e., conscious/preconscious/unconscious), perhaps we should draw the contrast between intentions which are explicitly described and those intentions which likewise govern behavior but resist verbalization. For example, if X hates Y, we could say either that X's true feelings are mysteriously hidden from him or that the feelings harbored by X are not acknowledged as feelings of hostility. Freud's remark that Elizabeth's legs would "join in the conversation" was intended to show how she obliquely expressed in neurotic symptoms a feeling which required further interpretation. The significance of Elizabeth's "comment," Freud learned, was at odds with her verbal description of her relevant past—what she did and why she did it. Therapy moved toward a resolution when Elizabeth noted that her pains became violent upon receiving word that her sister was deathly ill. As she repeated in therapy the symbolic response to the circumstances in which her illness originated, Elizabeth confessed that at her sister's deathbed her only thought was: "Now he is free again and I can be his [her brother-in-law's] wife."[34]

Was Elizabeth unable to report her innermost desires because they were mysteriously hidden from the person who had these feelings or rather because a verbal description of them would conflict with her moral convictions? The latter alternative leaves open the possibility that an analysand has intentions and beliefs which she does not acknowledge and that these intentions and beliefs find expression in her actions. As Olafson observes, such intentions may then be "either ignored or systematically misdescribed by the agent in terms of intentions and beliefs that [she] *is* willing to acknowledge both publicly and privately and which, as rationalizations of actions, are extensionally equivalent to the unacknowledged beliefs and intentions or approximately so."[35]

The extension of the vocabulary of action to "latent" dream thoughts or "unconscious" intentions would dismantle the clumsy apparatus of Freud's metapsychology and avoid the reification of thoughts and emotions which fall outside the range of normal consciousness. As attractive as this tactic may be, the transposition of manifest/latent into manifest/immanent flattens the crucial topographical distinction between preconscious and unconscious, a distinction justified by the phenomenon of banishment or exclusion of ideas from conscious life as well as by the clinical exigency to *infer* from gaps or lacunae in the patient's report the "missing" content subject to distortion by displacement or condensation.[36] If the metapsychological construct of the unconscious creates the problem of an intentionality which does not operate at the level of a first-person subjectivity, it is at the same time necessary as a means of explaining the function of repression and its reversal through the interpretive method of treatment.

The key question for our purpose is epistemological in nature. If we abandon the idea of unconsciously *retained* ideas, what value does psychoanalysis have as a *historical* explanation? Herbert Fingarette and others have argued that psychoanalysis enables an analysand to construct a history but that this task shares nothing in common with the attempt to match the explanation of the analyst with the enduring psychical formations of the analysand. Insight, more specifically, is a reorganization of the meaning of *present* experience, a present reorientation toward both past and future. "The patient in insight therapy plays a role analogous to that of the reader of the poem: what the patient reads are the bits and pieces of his life. He brings these fragments of his life to the therapist who then suggests a meaning scheme in terms of which to reorganize and unify the patient's experience."[37] According to Fingarette, known or memorable events of the past along with associated feelings and thoughts can be construed within a pattern of meanings which makes more of a unity than the meaning patterns the analysand had formerly used.

Belief in the possible intelligibility of events differs greatly from the conviction that an original idea has been lost or hidden by distortion. Freud pondered this alternative to his inspectionist view of "unconscious memories" in *Studies on Hysteria:*

> Even when everything is finished and the patients have been overborne by the force of logic and have been convinced by the therapeutic effect accompanying the emergence of precisely these ideas—when I say the patients themselves accept the fact that they have thought of this or that, they often add: "But I can't remember having thought it." *It is easy to come to terms with them by telling them that the thoughts were unconscious.* But

how is this state of affairs to be fitted into our own psychological views? Are we to disregard the withholding of recognition on the part of the patients, when, now that the work is finished, there is no longer any motive for their doing so? *Or are we to suppose that we are really dealing with thoughts which never came about, which merely had a possibility of existing, so that the treatment would lie in the accomplishment of a physical act which did not take place at the time?* [Emphasis mine.][38]

How can an interpretation be validated if there is no presumption of an originally, or unconsciously, formulated experience which the analysand must "remember" and which the analyst's interpretation must match? Freud's query raises the possibility that truth is not only insufficient to effect a therapeutic improvement but, more disturbingly, that "truth" is not even *necessary* for therapeutic efficacy. It is possible that therapeutic efficacy, while not correlated with the truth or accuracy of the narrative, is related to its adequacy, that is, its internal consistency, comprehensiveness, and coherence. Following Kermode, I have stressed that there seems to be a basic "rationalizing drive" in human experience, a need to see one's own behavior as forming a reasonable and meaningful pattern. Freud implied that a coherent story promotes mental health and that illness fragments the sense of one's own history. The adequate psychoanalytic narrative, by providing such a pattern—a reorganization of meaning—satisfies this need, thereby ameliorating the patient's anxiety and suffering. One possible implication might be that psychoanalytic explanations provide "necessary fictions" which function only therapeutically. If this is indeed its purpose, questions about veracity would be senseless, a misconstrual of the purpose served by the "talking cure."

We will return to the question of accuracy, the scientific significance of psychoanalytic statements, in the next chapter. However, it should be stressed that the problem of psychoanalysis is not only to edit the patient's report by revealing its untold significance in the etiology of the illness but to help the patient "reemplot" his or her life history by adjusting the value of the relevant past to the economy of events that make up his or her life. The analysand is troubled by symptoms and memories which he or she cannot coordinate within a unified, meaningful story. Psychoanalysis detraumatizes repressed memories and associations by assimilating them into a plot in which past incidents, however painful, can be made to play a minor role as tokens of a stage of life which has passed.

In undertaking the compilation of a life history, the therapist uncovers the archaeology of the subject; but he or she is also engaged in an enterprise oriented toward alleviating human suffering. The patient must not only "remember" the past but transcend it: "One works to the best of one's power as an elucidator where ignorance has given rise to fear, as a teacher, as the representative of a freer or superior view of the world, as a father confessor who gives absolution, as it were, by a continuance of his sympathy and respect after the confessions have been made."[39]

The story of illness and the determining power of the events at its source have their common end in the resolution of neurotic symptoms during the therapy hour. Freud's case histories draw the narrator into the story by plotting the dialogue in which both patient and therapist move, often in spite of one another and themselves, from ignorance to knowledge. Each party assists the other in the assigned task—the therapist in the patient's struggle against "forgetfulness," the patient in the therapist's reconstruction of the seemingly random fragments of his or her life. The case history thus represents a work in progress, a work of analysis which cannot be written until therapy has been terminated in the resolution and understanding of the patient's illness.

History and Science

I have noted affinities between historical inquiry as practiced by Freud and poetic works as understood by Aristotle. The two are comparable because they both dramatize human action and in doing so reveal essential truths about character and conflict. Aristotle rejected such a comparison, since past contingent events evince no intelligible order except by virtue of the conceptual scheme that the historian, in retrospect, illicitly imposes upon them. Historians, in other words, fail to do their job when they assume the role of storyteller. I have maintained, contrary to Aristotle, that literature and historical inquiry do share a commitment to storytelling as the narrative mode of following human action through time, specifically by reference to the intentional character of the desires, beliefs, and motives which shape the development and outcome of an agent's/character's peculiar story.

Has Freud managed to raise history to the level of a science? This question actually contains two issues: the compatibility of Freud's narrative commitment with scientific exploration, and the accuracy of his narrative accounts of neurotic illness. Although these issues are interrelated, I will address the question of evidence only after examining in what sense, if at all, Freud's narratives merit scientific status.

What Freud construed as the material of his investigation depended upon what he advanced, explicitly or by implication, as a criterion of knowledge. His essentially ambivalent attitude toward science—on the one hand, his wish to extend the rigor of scientific method, exemplified by physics, to the study of the mind, and his insistence that physical factors governed by regular laws of motion do not satisfactorily explain mental illness on the other—was heightened by his clinical posture toward the analysand and his or her disease. How we study humankind, as pointed out earlier, has moral as well as "purely scientific" consequences. By relegating neuroses to the medical domain, we deny the moral significance of symptoms and treat the patient as little more than a natural object that hosts the disease. However, once we recognize that the host is the disease, the study of neuroses cannot ignore the somewhat indefinite, imprecise domain of human action, character, and purpose.

The problem of what qualifies as a method of science therefore dovetails with the question of what counts as the subject matter of scientific study. This connection can be shown in Freud, whose dialectical and physical methods often operate simultaneously, by comparing psychoanalytical detective work with the task of assembling a jigsaw puzzle, where the individual pieces and their interrelationships represent the "material itself."[40] A jigsaw puzzle can be assembled by attending solely to the shape of the various pieces and their geometrical configuration: the convex fits into the concave. Or we can arrange the pieces according to pictorial-conceptual clues that suggest how each part contributes to the thematic representation exhibited by the picture as a whole. Although the relationship between two interlocking bits could be shown without reference to the depicted scene, we would be hard-pressed to communicate the relationship between pieces that are not adjacent to one another except in terms of representational associations. Conceptual representations, which I have discussed in terms of narrative frame of reference, play an important theoretical role in organizing the concrete, individual "bits" of historical experience.

Of course, the questionable supposition underlying the jigsaw puzzle analogy is that all the pieces are available to the player and they can all be thematically connected and ordered in a fully intelligible whole. This assumption actually mirrors Freud's confidence that the analysand's associations—apparently accidental, unconnected, and meaningless—ultimately cohere in a complete clinical picture of the patient's history. It is worth noting that Freud's free-association method, only hinted at in his earliest case histories, was inspired by an essay by Ludwig Börne instructing the reader how to become an effective writer of fiction. The essay, titled "On the Art of Becoming an Original Writer in Three Days," concludes with these words:

> Here follows the practical prescription I promised. Take a few sheets of paper and for three days in succession write down, without any falsification or hypocrisy, everything that comes into your head. Write what you think of yourself, your women, of the Turkish War, of Goethe, of the Fonk criminal case, of the Last Judgement, of those senior to you in authority—and when the three days are over you will be amazed at what novel and startling thoughts have welled up in you. That is the art of becoming an original writer in three days.[41]

Just as Börne had believed that all seemingly random thoughts of the day evince an order—one might say plot—when submitted to the powers of imagination, so Freud thought that all the ostensibly irrelevant thoughts of his patients were guided and determined by failed efforts at defense against painful memories; they were actually intermediate links in the chain of associations "between the idea from which we start and the pathogenic idea which we are in search of." Or, in a more elaborate puzzle, "it may be an idea which forms the starting point of a new series of thoughts and recollections at the end of which the pathogenic ideal will be found."[42]

What possible advantage might Freud gain by turning the bits colored side down so that only the geometric method could be applied in putting together the puzzle? How can neurotic illness be made intelligible without attending to how the ensemble of symptoms, memories, and associations represent the pattern of meaning in the patient's history? Again, scientific expectations and methods generally harmonize with the idea one holds about what constitutes scientific knowledge. As the elements of his universal physics, Descartes chose geometrical figures devoid of secondary qualities which extend the clarity and certainty of mathematics to nature.

Freud's description of the psychic apparatus as a nervous economy combined the ideal of a system of purely structural features with content from Locke's psychology. Locke maintained in his account of human understanding that sensory impulses transmitted from the nerves to the brain are the ultimate sources of mental and affective life. Freud grafted the Newtonian principle of the conservation of energy upon a corpuscular or physiological conception of mental life—including psychopathology—thus reducing the diversity of human action to the distribution of "quanta" according to known laws of physiological motion.

This account of the mind differs sharply from Freud's case histories, in which a deep connection exists between subjectivity and the narrative order of literature. When faced with perplexing behavior, the analyst is not troubled by a gap in his or her neurological understanding but by an incongruity between the patient's intentions and actions. The Cartesian method of explanation was attractive to Freud because it promised the extension of a formal, deductive procedure to the realm of human affairs. But this kind of explanation simply does not fit with what needed explaining. The narrativizing character of human lives resists reduction to the metric ordering of time. As Kermode has observed, the mind has a propensity to discern through forward and backward syntheses a unity of meaning, where the passage of time is no longer "just one damned thing after another."[43] Stories, in other words, have beginnings and endings that pattern the flow of time by introducing continuity and purpose which overcome the mere successiveness of discrete moments in chronological time.

Puzzles, of course, are usually put together by attending to *both* pictorial cues and structural configurations of the various bits. Freud, as we shall see shortly, was trying to do much the same thing when he offered etiological equations which organized his clinical observations of how hysterics developed neurotic symptoms. Yet he seemed uncertain about how to compose storytelling and scientific explanation. At one moment he would maintain that repression was the work of symbolization, but then he would draw back: "Hysterical repression clearly takes place by the help of symbolization. It might be supposed that the riddle lies in this displacement . . . but we shall find that [in obsessional neurosis] repression occurs without symbolization. . . . Accordingly, the process of repression remains the core of the riddle."[44]

Throughout his career, Freud tried to solve his riddle, periodically returning to his early representation of mental life as "quantitatively determined states of specific material particles," as he wrote in the "Scientific Project." At the same time, he knew that the attempt to quantify mental life ultimately demanded the use of metaphorical models, precisely the poetic language that he sought to purge from his "rigorous" science. Reflecting on the linguistic medium of psychoanalysis, Freud consciously shifted back and forth between his empirical and literary casts of mind:

> We are obliged to operate with scientific terms, that is to say with the figurative language, peculiar to psychology. . . . We could not otherwise describe the processes at all, and indeed question at all, and indeed we could not have become aware of them. . . . [Though] the deficiencies in our description would probably

vanish if we were already in a position to replace the psychological terms by physiological or chemical ones, it is true that these too are only part of a figural language.[45]

The Covering Law Theory

The temptation to eliminate narrative exegesis from his reflections arose from Freud's implicit assumption that an explanation, regardless of its subject matter, must conform to the deductive and experimental methods of the natural sciences. Are these methods adequate to the task of demonstrating how hysterical symptoms are "determined"? Freud's use of the latter term appears to rest on the Kantian conception of nature as the totality of events connected by Newtonian laws; causally determined events, in turn, exhaust the realm of what is knowable. Given this account of nature—and human nature—Freud's investigation of psychoneuroses would possess explanatory power only if the case history could logically deduce symptomatic effects from causal laws.

Carl Hempel, a positivist who originally formulated the covering law model, tried to demonstrate that what constitutes an explanation in history is the logical deduction of a singular statement from a general covering law, or combination of laws, and a statement of initial conditions.[46] A simple example would be the explanation of why my radiator cracked. If we can formulate laws governing the behavior of water under certain atmospheric conditions and specify such initial conditions as the temperature on a given night and the materials from which the radiator was made, then we can logically derive the singular statement that the radiator cracked. Further, I can predict that whenever these conditions are met the same phenomenon will occur.

As an example of how his covering law model could encompass historical phenomena, Hempel referred to the successive positions of a stone in free flight:

> Even successive stages in a physical phenomenon such as free
> flight of a stone may be regarded as forming a genetic sequence

whose different stages—characterized, let us say, by the position and the velocity of the stone at different times—are interconnected by strictly universal laws, and the successive stages in the movement of a steel ball bouncing in zig zags down a Dalton Board may be regarded as forming a genetic sequence with probablistic connections.[47]

This is a misleading illustration of *historical* explanation for three reasons. First, Hempel distorts the meaning of a "genetic sequence" by implying that the unfolding of a historical episode is reducible to discrete objects located at separate points in time. The following form of explanation indicates how E-like events follow C-like events without elucidating the transaction between initial conditions and their consequences: "In every case where an event of a specified kind C occurs at a certain time and place, an event of a specified kind E will occur at a place and a time which is related to the place and time of the occurrence of the first specified event."[48] The narrativist defines a historical event as a temporal whole, a pattern in which initial conditions are embedded in subsequent events. The decisive question, one neglected by Hempel, is precisely how one event *generates* or leads to another through a process of internal development. Danto makes this point when he writes, "The events in question are connected as endpoints of a temporally extended change—as the beginning and end of a temporal whole—and it is the change thus indicated for which a cause is sought."[49]

The second weakness in Hempel's model concerns his related assumption that historical events may be understood as homogeneous members of a class covered by a general description. Scientific explanation seeks to understand *classes* of events—all radiators on all nights—rather than particular, nonrepeatable events that resist classification. If history is not cognitively empty or unscientific, then historical explanation must show by means of regularities how one event is causally connected with others in its "genetic" chain. Yet it is precisely the specific connection between particular causes and particular effects that begs for explanation; and this relationship can be captured adequately only in a fully articulated narrative.

Hempel's most dubious assumption is that explanation is secured by predictive power. Historical inquiry is stimulated by questions about particular episodes that did in fact happen, and the function of historical explanation is to judge their significance with the advantage of hindsight. Of course, these objections do not decide the issue of whether Freud's claims should be judged according to the canons of scientific method as defined by Hempel or by the narrativist criteria for an adequate historical explanation. Assuming the validity of the covering law model in explaining natural phenomena, would we be correct in applying it to Freud's psychoanalytic material as well? Throughout his early psychological writings, Freud developed various etiological equations for understanding the pathogenesis of psychoneuroses. The terms of his equations were intended to enable the analyst to deduce from a logical formula the conditions which must be satisfied for the appearance of a specific form of neurosis. The four causes cited in one of Freud's more elaborate studies were: precondition, specific cause, concurrent cause, and precipitating or releasing cause.[50]

Although Freud eventually decided that hereditary taint need not enter into the etiology of neuroses, in his paper "Heredity and the Etiology of Hysteria" (1896) he maintained that it is an indispensable precondition for the occurrence of the illness in question. Without a predisposition to neurosis, no acquired cause could produce neurotic symptoms. However, the precondition is not sufficient to trigger neuroses, since they must be accompanied by a specific cause in the predisposed person. Moreover, because heredity enters into the etiology of all defense neuroses, the precondition could not determine the specific form or type which the illness might take.

Specific causes were said to determine the "choice" of neurosis. Each neurosis, Freud believed, has its source in "a special disturbance of the nervous economy," and these "pathological functional changes betray, as their common source, the sexual life of the person concerned, either a disturbance in his present life or important events in his past life."[51] As mentioned earlier, Freud postulated a special etiological relationship between the nature of the sexual factor and the choice of neurosis, dividing the latter into two major clinical types: the current neuroses such as neurasthenia and anxiety neurosis, which derive from the physiological or toxicological consequences of abnormally high or low levels of sexual (somatic) tension associated with masturbation, continence, coitus interruptus, and other sexual practices, and the psychoneuroses, subdivided into two principal syndromes—hysteria and obsessional neurosis—according to the nature of past incidents in one's sexual life and the subsequent mode of defense against memories of the traumatic scene. In hysteria, defense takes place when the "affect" attached to the sexual ideas is channeled into some bodily form of expression; whereas in obsessional neurosis the quantity of affect attaches to another, nonsexual idea. Both "conversion" and "transposition" were described by Freud as mechanisms by which the nervous system "distributes excitation" in order to restore equilibrium.

Such maladies as physical exhaustion, traumatic illness, and mental excitement were essential to the etiological equations of Breuer and Charcot. But Freud believed that they play an ancillary role which only hastens the appearance of an illness. Finally, the precipitating or proximate cause referred to a specific event or incident which immediately results in the development of sexual symptoms; for example, a sexual experience which activates the memory of a childhood trauma.

Carlyle remarked that those features of reality which cannot be repeated are by nature the material of the historian.[52] If this is so, and Freud's equations purported to state general laws governing abnormal behavior, then it is difficult to see how etiological explanations could possibly capture the material identified with the analysand's historical past. Etiology aims at stating the general and timeless conditions under which all possible instances of a given neurosis would occur, as well as serving the taxonomic aim of putting the various neuroses into their respective types of categories. In this respect the psychologist resembles the naturalist whose "history of the whale" attends to individuals only as instances of a type. "The history of the whale," George Dennis O'Brien observes, "is a history of the species, not of named individuals. From the standpoint of nature and the naturalist, the individual repeats the type, and anything which calls attention to the particularity of this individual runs contrary to the interests of the scientist and the 'interest' of nature in preserving the type."[53] Indeed, as we saw in Aristotle's poetics, the individual qua individual falls into the category of accident, since the value of a dramatic or scientific work would be diminished if *this* individual deviated from others in the same species. But if the naturalist's purpose is to identify variations that distinguish the development and habits of individuals within a particular group, species classification may frame inquiry but no longer can advance it.

Kant acknowledged that meaning, purpose, or action cannot be comprehended by the laws which govern humankind as part of a larger natural order. Because humans alone act as individuals, the core concept of which is Reason (*Vernunft*) conceived as self-determination, they enjoy a kind of dignity which place them outside the realm of nature. However, as a consequence, the individuality or agency of humans which escapes determination cannot, by definition, be knowable. Purposefulness for Kant was how we understand, not what we understand. In Kant's own language, purpose is the form of a subject's reflection, not the determination of an object. If the aim of psychoanalysis is to reconstruct the psychic history of individuals in order to recover the sense of their neurotic action, then we are still left with the formidable task of distinguishing the "nature" of history from the nature of nature without presuming that historical inquiry lacks the explanatory power or integrity usually reserved for the sciences.

Psychoanalysts, I have suggested, are interested in explaining their subject matter in all its particularity, in accounting for all those features which make it distinct from other objects or events of a similar nature. Far from disregarding those aspects which fail to conform to typical classes or patterns of disturbed behavior, the opposite is nearer the truth. It is precisely the peculiarities of that behavior which appear to be incongruous and call for an explanation. Yet the subject matter of psychoanalysis is not individual bits of behavior either. Psychoanalytic explanation offers a general account of a specific life, the peculiar patterns of behavior that constitute an individual's history. The explanation of a particular dream or compulsive idea is situated in the larger story which organizes and illuminates an individual life. To state my point in Hegelian terms, the explanations of history should mediate between brute particularity that borders on the ineffable and the vanishing of events into universal laws. Neither raw description nor Hempel's covering law model will suffice.

Determining and Overdetermining

We are now prepared to take a second look at the sense in which neurotic symptoms are determined. The etiological equation indicates that hysteria has no single cause but can be traced to a whole set of factors which only together are causally sufficient. "The principal factors in the aetiology of neuroses," wrote Freud, "is that their genesis is as a rule overdetermined (überdeterminiert), that several factors must come together to produce this result."[54] Although etiology specifies relevant causal factors, it does not suffice as an explanation, since there is a logical gap between theory and previous experience on the one hand and the individual patient on the other. This can be seen clearly by turning to Roland Dalbeiz's example of a patient who repeated one hundred times: "I am the king of Russia, Garibaldi is my uncle, the pope is my grandfather," with a final phrase on which she laid great emphasis, "I am the child of the old commode."[55] A careful physician who studied the development of the symptoms would conclude, according to Dalbiez, that her "affective indifference and radical disharmony" indicated hebephrenic-catatonic schizophrenia. The accuracy of the diagnosis does not really concern us here. What the example illustrates is the omission of any inquiry into the sense or intelligibility of specific symptoms. Why does the patient call herself the child of the old commode rather than of the old table or the old cupboard? The statement of conditions necessary for the onset of the illness (e.g., sexual trauma coupled with hereditary predisposition) cannot comprehend the illness, since the

task of interpreting the meaning of symptoms moves from these
generalities to the specific circumstances in which the symptoms arose, as well as their function and significance within the
economy of the patient's mental life.

Freud intimated a second sense of overdetermination which
referred not to a plurality of discrete causal factors but to the
case history as an associative structure analogous to a text:

> To relate [the explanation of a single symptom] in detail would
> occupy the whole period of this lecture. The chain of association
> always has more than two links and the traumatic scenes do not
> form a simple row, like a string of pearls, but ramify and are
> interconnected like genealogical trees, so that in any new experi-
> ence two or more earlier come into operation as memories. In
> short, *giving an account of the resolution of a single symptom*
> *would in fact amount to the task of relating an entire case histo-*
> *ry.* [Emphasis mine.][56]

Although Freud cautioned against abstracting from the whole
of the case history in order to elucidate any single part of it, an
example drawn from one of his clinical studies illustrates both
why he could not rely on an exclusively causal mode of explanation and how language enters into psychoanalysis as the
chief (over)determinant of neurotic symptomatology. In his
analysis of a rat phobia, the patient's most acute obsessional
symptom, Freud gained an understanding of the patient's behavior through the following linguistic associations: *Ratten* =
rat; *Raten* = installments; *Spielratte* = gambler.[57] The history
of the "Rat Man" was organized around this verbal puzzle—the
pun *Ratten*—whose overdeterminations were unpacked to reveal the associative structure of the patient's repressed material. The patient, Freud learned, originally associated "rat"
with his father when he detected what appeared to be a rat
crawling along the top of his father's grave. From further associations Freud also discerned the patient's identification with
his father-soldier and the simultaneous rebellion against such
identification and shame over the father's gambling (*Spielratte*)
and his "crime" of failing to repay a debt (*Raten*). The patient's
report of his past and free associations, coupled with the de-

formed language of his rat phobia, suggested a kind of grammar which revealed to Freud the motivation behind his otherwise incongruous actions and beliefs.

Again, we see how words give a specific form to a symptom through symbolization; the example also shows how the recovery of "lost words" translates the private language of neurotic symptoms into the public speech of the therapeutic narrative. The overdetermination of the analysand's symptoms reinforces the thesis, stated at the beginning of this chapter, that, because of the irreducibly linguistic quality of psychopathology, the "object" as well as the method of psychoanalysis must be regarded as a text rather than a natural fact.

If etiology cannot offer an adequate account of the individual case, neither can psychoanalysis supply a set of well-confirmed interpretive rules for unpacking the meaning of individual symptoms or dreams. Although analysts possess rules of thumb, these should not be construed as determinants of what happens but as surmises to make what happens more intelligible or as guidelines to pursue a particular line of inquiry. The rules of interpretation are not akin to hypotheses which confirm or disconfirm the inevitability of an event but function as normative hypotheses that can guide inquiry into why events did or did not unfold as expected. Dale Porter notes that such hypotheses can direct us to patterns of continuity and change, suggest pertinent variables when comparing events with their antecedents, or identify dispositions—characteristic patterns of behavior—that help explain the outcome of a sequence of events in which an agent participates.[58] Louis Mink neatly summarizes this difference between the scientific and historical senses of "hypothesis" when he writes, "For the scientist, the hypothesis is the target; for the historian, a signpost. . . . In Kantian language, one might say that hypotheses as rules for inquiry are constitutive in science, regulative in history."[59]

Although the analyst's rules, or normative hypotheses, can guide inquiry, they cannot guarantee its success precisely because what constitutes an explanation varies according to the context of interpretation. Michael Sherwood makes the point that "there is no characteristic of logic or grammar through which explanatory power is assured. Rather, the answer must always be found in the situation within which the statement is made, the context within which the statement functions, and the way in which it is used."[60] Freud similarly disdained a priori explanatory rules when he challenged the view that dream elements could be decoded as if they were fixed universal symbols rather than context-dependent tokens of a particular life: "My procedure," he wrote, "is not so convenient as the popular decoding method which translates any given piece of a dream's content by a fixed key. I, on the contrary, am prepared to find that the same occurs in various people or in a different context."[61]

A language cannot be understood or exhausted by cataloging the words that fill its lexicon. Each word gains its sense only in and through its relationship to other signs. Consequently, the explanation of incongruities in the patient's life would derive in each case from the network of significance reconstructed in the therapy hour. The reader may find one interpretation compelling, another farfetched (when, for example, the punning ground rules strain credulity), but in both cases the process of Freud's inferences cannot be described as a formal procedure comparable to that recommended by Hempel. In place of a method that can be correctly or incorrectly applied, psychoanalytic interpretation depends on the talent of the analyst who gives a "reading" which satisfies our desire for intelligibility. As A. R. Louch notes, such an explanation "depends wholly on the person making the inferences and he is evaluated wholly in terms of his success."[62]

This characterization of psychoanalytic narrative seems applicable to historical explanation generally considered. The chief difference between the explanations of the natural sciences and those of history is that the historian's conclusions are exhibited in the texture of the entire narrative rather than demonstrated as the outcome in a series of deductive steps. Mink makes this important point by distinguishing between "ingredient" and "detachable" conclusions:

> Detachable conclusions are possible in science because—and only because—of its theoretical structure. But despite the fact that a historian may "summarize" conclusions in his final chap-

ter, it seems clear that these are seldom or never detachable conclusions; not merely their validity but their meaning refers backward to the ordering of evidence in the total argument. The significant conclusions, one might say, are ingredient in the argument itself . . . *represented by the narrative order itself.*[63]

The ideal of explanation, as Hempel understood the term, is here replaced by the reconstruction of the whole story, which necessarily goes beyond the fragments of the patient's report but also must depart from and return to the individual's assorted memories and associations. Each fragment finds its place in a tangled skein that attains order and meaning only in the analyst's edited narrative. Freud made this claim for psychoanalytic narratives in his own rendering of the picture puzzle analogy.

Just as when putting together children's picture puzzles, we finally after many attempts become absolutely certain which piece belongs to the gap not yet filled—because only that particular piece at the same time completes the puzzle and can be fitted with irregular edges to the edges of other pieces in such a way as neither to leave space nor to overlap—so the content of the infantile scenes proves to be an inevitable completion of the associative and logical structure of the neurosis; and only after they have been inserted does its origins become evident—one might say self-evident.[64]

Although he remained bewitched by a preconceived notion of scientific method, Freud's inquiry into the intentions disguisedly expressed by memory symbols and his comparison of narrative construction with the decipherment of an ancient script suggested a model of understanding more akin to the acquisition or translation of a language than the prediction and control of human behavior under a system of natural laws. And the necessity of Freud's explanation derived not from the universality or predictive value of his findings but from their narrative continuity and coherence. In this connection Aristotle's notion of internal necessity bears repeating: "an imitation of one action, a complete whole with its several incidents so closely connected that the transposal or withdrawal of one will disjoin and dislocate the whole."[65]

3

Psychoanalysis as
Science Fiction

In Freud's picture puzzle analogy, the seduction scene functioned as the "self-evident" piece needed to complete the narrative structure. The analogy was misleading, however, since the conclusion exhibited or demanded by the plot proved to be at once compelling and fantastic. After formulating an etiology of neuroses based on the reality of the seduction scenes, Freud came to suspect that what his patients had been reporting as historically accurate memories were actually imaginative fictions. "Scenes from early infancy, such as are brought up by an exhaustive analysis of neuroses . . . are not always reproductions of real occurrences, to which it is possible to ascribe an influence over the course of the patient's later life and over the formation of his symptoms. Rather, they are frequently products of the imagination."[1]

In the preceding chapter, I suggested that Freud's case studies shared with imaginative writing a dramatic structure, not that psychoanalysis was itself a fictional genre. Although the case study may be regarded as a narrative reconstruction exhibiting the development and unity of a short story, Freud insisted that psychoanalysis, like any respectable science and unlike works of fiction, must offer sufficient evidence to justify its stories. His discovery that the "self-evident" seduction scenes never occurred demonstrated the importance of matching the reconstructed text with evidence external to the intentional structure of experiences recollected or reenacted by the patient. The text of the illness undoubtedly required interpretation, but the reading of dreams and symptoms demanded validation as well, particularly since the patient's report about his or her remote past was vulnerable to distortion and misrepresentation.

Although history is necessarily more than the chronicling of discrete events, the move from sense to reference, from the internal exigencies of the plot to corroboration of claims of truth by evidence, requires that certain substantial events *did* occur, occurred in *this* sequence, this time and place. In other words, confirmation of what is depicted within the narrative must come from the outside, from the reality elucidated or dramatized by the plot. One of Freud's chief epistemological assumptions about the nature of reality was, indeed, its externality. "And we are confronted with the task of development of the relation of neurotics and of mankind in general to reality, and in this way of bringing the psychological significance of the real external world into the structure of our theories."[2]

The identification of reality with the external world supplied Freud with a standard of mental health and a criterion for distinguishing fantasy as a distortion of the real. His writings on the neuroses and dreams can be read as an il-logic of the imagination, a survey of the strategems which enable neurotics and dreamers alike to thwart reality by imaginatively denying or fulfilling their basic instinctual wishes. By comprehending the rules governing the emergence of fantasy and illusion, Freud hoped to present a historically accurate picture of the patient's illness as it stretched backward to its origin and forward to the scene of the therapy hour. His therapeutic program aimed at restoring to conscious memory the unconscious meaning of the apparently absurd symptom or dream by recovering the significance of events or scenes which instigated it. The final rendering of scenes responsible for the formation of neurotic symptoms thus claimed independence from fiction and fidelity to the stubborn facts. Even if fantasy figured in the patient's recollections, the perceptive analyst could eventually sort out what had been falsified from the determinate circumstances of the

patient's life. Hence, externality is doubly important as a criterion of reality in psychoanalysis: not only does recognition of
the outside world distinguish a "normal" individual who
adapts to reality from an "abnormal" one who repudiates it, but
the referential status of a case study also determines whether
the narrative tells the historical truth or merely concocts in-
ventive fictions.

The interpretation of reality as a specifically external realm,
one which is unbending in contrast to the world of fantasy, first
appeared in Freud's "Scientific Project." His early developmental theory maintained that differentiation between external and
internal stimuli forms the basis for all subsequent distinctions
between self and world. Dependent upon the care of others, the
infant can reduce the tension introduced by external stimuli
only by screaming for help ("specific action") or seeking hallucinatory wish-fulfillment. The early association of pain or dis-
appointment with an alien, external reality and pleasure with
the uninhibited play of the body leaves a lasting impression,
but children eventually learn that they cannot rely on another
person, flight, or projection to satisfy their basic needs. Consequently, the education of their ego begins with "reality testing" as a means of distinguishing what is externally real from
what has its source in their own wishes, that is, from heavily
cathected ideas of some desired object. By comparing representations of memory or imagination with perceptions, children
test the object of representation to see if it is "perceptually
identical" with the object of an external perception. This process introduces to the child's experience a dichotomy between
the inner world of the self represented in hallucination (a form
of imagination) and the external world apprehended by valid
perception (a form of knowledge). In Freud's words, reality testing serves "(the) function of orientating the individual in the
world by discriminating between what is internal [instincts, affects, thoughts, fantasies] and what is external [perceptual ob-
jects]."[3] When such discrimination or judgment becomes habit-
ual, Freud would say that the "reality principle" has held sway
over the "pleasure principle." Conversely, when fantasies and

wishes obstruct commerce with the external world, he would observe that an instance of regression has taken place, a reversion to the mode of functioning characteristic of children.

The above account rests on the familiar thesis that perception aided by judgment provides our sole access to reality insofar as it is knowable, and that the misapprehension of the world stems from the failure to discriminate between the real and what is only imagined or remembered. Hobbes made this claim in the *Leviathan* when he called fancy the faculty which discerns likeness and judgment the faculty which discerns differences. Of the two, he continued, "judgment, without the help of fancy, is commended for itself," but fancy "without steadiness and direction to some end is one great kind of madness."[4] Imagination, assigned a subordinate place among the faculties, may help a writer express his or her thoughts vividly but it is not in itself a rational activity. Hobbes did concede one exception to the rule that fancy has no place in strictly logical or scientific discourse: "In demonstration, in counsel, and all rigorous search of truth, judgment does all, except sometimes the understanding has need to be opened by some apt similitude; and then there is so much need for fancy."[5]

Freud similarly observed that although it is important for the analyst who interprets the illness to exercise careful judgment, the patient should "suppress his critical faculty." If he succeeds in doing that, "innumerable ideas come into his head of which he otherwise would not have gotten hold." Schiller is then quoted at length in a letter advising a friend who complained of his meager literary production:

> The ground for your complaint seems to me to lie in the constraint imposed upon your imagination. . . . It seems a bad thing and detrimental to the creative work of the mind if reason makes too close an examination of ideas as they come pouring in. Looked at in isolation, a thought may seem very trivial or very fantastic, but it may be made important by other thoughts that come after it, and, in conjunction with other thoughts that may seem equally absurd, it may turn out to form a more effective

link. Reason cannot form any opinion upon all this unless it retains the thought long enough to look at it in connection with the
others.[6]

Freud's remedy for writer's cramp recalls Hobbes's attempt to
link the association of ideas to the activity of imagination. The
power of fancy to relate similar images is enhanced, Hobbes
believed, by the mental habit of contiguous association, that is,
the ability of one image to recall another that has previously
been connected with it. Freud recognized that in the analysis of
a dream or symptom the free play of ideas recommended by
Schiller could provide both a stimulus to recollection and a
context in which to judge the relative significance of its elements. For example, through associations with parts of a
dream, the patient could penetrate its disguises; the associations would lead him or her from the deceptive "manifest content" of the remembered dream to the "latent content" where a
wish was invariably lodged. To the extent that free association
facilitated the backward flow of the patient's thoughts, it may be
said that Freud's procedure joined memory and imagination as
psychical partners. Hobbes, of course, went one step further in
asserting their identity: "They are but one thing which for divers considerations have divers names," differing only according
to whether more stress is placed upon the content of the "decaying *sense*" or upon the quality of decay.[7]

Although Locke followed Hobbes in recognizing two powers
of the mind—one which discerns resemblances between ideas,
the other differences—he regarded the power of the mind to
associate ideas as inherently dangerous. He was well aware that
people too often make irrational connections between ideas
and through repeated and false associations are habituated to
prejudice and error in their thinking. Since both memory and
imagination arise from the "decaying sense," the danger always
exists that past experiences will be distorted through the medium of recollection.[8]

Considered as an instrument of psychoanalysis, free association enriched the fund of clinical material and opened up perspectives on mental life that were unavailable by more restrictive methods. Yet he shared Locke's fear of the irrational

consequences of an imagination—whether the analyst's or analysand's—unchecked by judgment. Neurotics, according to Freud, suffer from the disease of false connections (*Falsche Verknupfungen*): "In cases in which the true causation evades conscious perception one does not hesitate to make another connection, which one believes, although it is false. What is recorded in conscious memory is not the relevant experience itself but another psychical element closely associated in time or space with the objectionable one [i.e., the weak sense of symbolization]."[9] This phenomenon of transference (*Übertragung*) appears in enactive memories as well as explicit recollections. For example, instead of offering recollections of his father's overbearing behavior toward him as a child, the patient might behave in the same fashion toward his son or analyst. The patient's reenactment of an earlier identification betrays his failure to distinguish himself as a rememberer from the content of his memory or the past from his present situation. Transference, issuing from the patient's compulsion to associate (*Assoziationzwang*), ignores the laws of contradiction and causality and shows a *lack of differentiation* between past and present, subject and object, internal and external.

Freud believed that reason could profit from its alliance with imagination provided that judgment permit us to differentiate the logical from the illogical, the true connection from the imagined one. "We are justified," he wrote, "in giving free reign to our speculation so long as we retain the coolness of our judgment and do not mistake the scaffolding for the building."[10] Theoretical fictions may help to organize scientific inquiry provided that they, like the patient's fantasies, are circumscribed and clearly distinguished from the latent, literal truth.

This chapter concerns the status of psychoanalysis as science fiction, a term which may refer either to a science of fictions—again, considered as a logic of imagination skillfully applied in clinical practice—or to a fictional science, one that has been infected with the very misrepresentations it has sought to expel through its teachings. The latter formulation brings to mind Pascal's disparaging view of the imagination as the mistress of falsehood and error. Is it possible that Freud, for all his coolness of judgment, was himself seduced by false connections, fictions which managed to escape his conscious control?

Traumatic Fictions

In his early papers on defense neuroses, Freud was faced with the difficult task of explaining why some adults who had suffered traumatic experiences remained healthy and, conversely, how a seemingly trivial experience could have sufficient traumatic power to induce hysterical symptoms. Because of this discrepancy, hysteria could not be made fully intelligible as the effect of a trauma coinciding with the first appearance of neurotic symptoms. Either the disposition to hysteria had already existed long before the trauma or the regressive method would have to delve more deeply into the patient's past to discover the event or scene responsible for the onset of the illness. A deeper probing of repressed material revealed to Freud that behind every later scene was an earlier and more traumatic event. The ultimate source of hysterical symptoms, he decided, was an overt sexual seduction. Sexual incidents after puberty were now viewed as traumas only insofar as they "awakened the psychical trace of the childhood event" and not because they activated a hereditary predisposition to the neurosis.[11]

When Freud first formulated his scenario of sexual seduction, he reasoned that hysteria is the consequence of a passive childhood event and obsessional neurosis the result of a subsequent active, pleasurable experience. Because he did not yet consider sexual precocity a natural phenomenon, Freud was convinced that a premature sexual awakening could occur only if the child were first the victim of a sexual assault by an adult. Once victimized, the child might then commit sexually aggressive acts toward other children. Self-reproaches due to feelings of guilt and shame would account for later obsessional symptoms which carry the burden of repressed childhood memories. The relationship between the pathogenic event and the course of the illness was more difficult to establish in the case of hysteria, since the nature of the trauma cast little light on why specifically somatic symptoms (e.g., paralysis) were eventually produced as a defense against memories of the trauma. In response to this problem, Freud proposed that the child's age at the time of the trauma, as well as the type of sexual encounter, might explain the "choice of neurosis." Specifically, he associated the pathogenic event in hysteria with an early stage of the child's mental development. Unable to form linguistic associations with events, the child would respond physically, rather than verbally, to all stimuli. The somatic conversions of hysteria might then be explained as regression to the primitive level of functioning characteristic of the child at the time of the original trauma.[12]

If the child is psychologically and physiologically immature and does not yet comprehend the *meaning* of sexuality, we may ask precisely in what sense the act of seduction constitutes a trauma and why the need for defense should ever arise. Freud replied that the seduction scene becomes traumatic only years after its occurrence, when the victim's memories resonate with a trivial postpubertal experience reminiscent (i.e., symbolic) of the infantile trauma. It was pointed out earlier that painful ideas ordinarily trigger normal inhibition by association with other, less painful, ideas or by weakening their affect through repetition in conscious memory. If *normal* defense is unnecessary for a child who unwittingly submits to sexual advances that he or she scarcely understands, then we would hardly expect *pathological* defense (i.e., repression) to ensue. Freud answered that what is traumatic, properly speaking, is not the event called the psychical trauma but the *memory* of the infantile experience, which releases unpleasure and induces repression: "The psychical trauma—or more precisely, the memory of the trauma—acts like a foreign body which long after its entry must be regarded as an agent that is still at work."[13]

This peculiar circumstance in which the memory of the seduction generates more unpleasure than the original experience was related by Freud to the fact that puberty has intervened between the event and reminiscence. "A sexual event in one phase," he wrote, "acts in the next phase as though it were a current one and at the same time uninhibitable."[14] Only in the case of a sexual event does the magnitude of affect increase as time passes. The effect of the seduction, deferred until puberty, takes the ego by surprise, thus triggering abnormal defense long after the so-called trauma has taken place.

> A memory excites an affect which it had not excited as an experience, because in the meantime the changes produced by puberty had made possible a new understanding of what was remembered. Now this case is typical of repression hysteria. We invariably find that a memory is repressed which had only become a trauma after the event. The reason for this state of things is the retardation of puberty as compared with the remainder of the individual development.[15]

Under Charcot's tutelage and later in his collaboration with Breuer, Freud based his psychological explanation of hysteria on the model of an emotionally painful event of external origin which directly released somatic effects. The trauma was said to have taken place in the patient's past as the cause of the illness and as the ultimate source of all symptoms connected with the disease. Freud's scenario of seduction thus confirmed his belief that sexuality, trauma, and repression were inextricably linked in the etiology of psychoneuroses.

Although the principle of deferred action (Nächtraglichkeit) strengthened Freud's claim that neurotics suffer from reminiscences, it also transformed the meaning of "trauma" and made the notion of historical origins highly problematical. One major weakness of the seduction theory was that it left unexplained how the passivity of the child's role in a sexual overture could be reconciled with the intellectual activity necessary for the child to acknowledge and absorb the experience as something worth remembering. Why, in other words, would the initial experience leave a trace—whether conscious or unconscious—if the child were incapable of appreciating the act's sexual significance as it occurred? Freud reasoned that the child's incapacity for putting ideas into words was a necessary condition for the onset of hysteria, just as the capacity for translating the memory of the experience was a necessary condition for lifting repression and resolving the neurotic symptoms.

We can see that in accounting for the specifically deferred effects of the primary trauma, Freud introduced another knotty problem. If the signification is not forgotten, then it becomes unclear just what leaves its trace in memory, resurfaces in puberty, and subsequently undergoes repression. Common sense tells us that the intensity of the memory and its related symptoms derive from the signification—the translation into words—associated with the relevant childhood event. But this account would leave unexplained the choice of neurosis. Again, the theory argued that specifically somatic symptoms would ensue only if the child were incapable of signifying the traumatic event qua "trauma" at the time it occurred. This conceptual move put Freud in an awkward position as a clinician because the interpretation of symptoms always betrays a verbal reworking of earlier significations, word associations that the theory would make unintelligible.[16]

Here lies the tension in psychoanalytic narrative between "what actually happened" and the patient's report. If anamnesis is a source of psychoanalytic knowledge, the problem is not merely one of identifying distortions of memory due to repression but of explaining the very *possibility* of childhood memories when a logical gap exists between what the patient remembers and how he remembers.[17] Can the "event" of seduction occur without a registration of significance at the time and, if not, should we say the seduction is not a discrete historical event which occurred independently of the patient's current associations but, instead, as the product of narrative reconstruction?

The ambiguity of Freud's seduction theory arises from the peculiarity that a trauma implies the existence of at least two events separated by a wide temporal interval. His etiological explanation sought to understand neuroses by demonstrating the priority and determining power of discrete events, but hysteria was now structured as a dialectic of presence and absence in which the origin was no longer reducible to a simple, substantial event. An explanation was achieved only by situating the trauma in the "play of deceit" (*Proton Pseudos*) between two scenes, neither of which was sexual or traumatic in itself.

In the case of Emmy von N., for example, a repressed childhood scene was sexual for the merchant who was said to have seduced her but not for Emmy, at least not at the time that it happened. The second—and consciously remembered—scene, dating from age twelve or thirteen, occurred when Emmy went into a store, saw two merchants laughing, and rushed out in a state of fright.[18] Although the later incident seemed to contain no sexual significance, Emmy believed it was the origin of her phobia concerning stores. The second scene was traumatic for Emmy but not for the shopkeepers or impartial witnesses to the incident. And the childhood scene, if her memory is to be trusted, was sexual for the merchant but not for her, at least not until the scene was linked to her adolescent trauma. One scene cannot be isolated as the straightforward cause and origin of a genetic sequence that leads directly to another later scene. In the case of Emmy, it is precisely the later scene that displaces the "origin" and gives it, in turn, a "derived" status. Each scene is implied and necessitated by the other as something which both exceeds its counterpart and suffers an insufficiency that the other event must supplement: the first scene lacked traumatic power, the second scene lacked sexual content; the first scene exceeded the second in content, the second exceeded the first in sexual significance. This dialectic, made possible by the peculiar temporal character of human development, disturbs the notion of the "material itself" or "historical facts," for the history of Emmy's illness was itself a thematic construction that resisted the attempt to isolate an unambiguous cause or primal scene occurring outside and behind the ensemble of memories and linguistic associations of the patient.

Philosophic questions concerning linguistic signification and reference, the contextual production of meaning, and the definition of psychical reality—questions only hinted at so far—would later prey on Freud's mind, but at the time Emmy's case was written, the principle of deferred action was envisioned as the saving argument for the traumatic etiology. Even so, he remained sensitive to the need for a means of segregating patients' deferred memories from their merely retrospective imaginings. If we are limited to the testimony of belatedly traumatic memories—memories that are traumatic only after the fact—how can we manage to fix the traumatic event historically? How can we be certain that the patient has not merely projected present desires or aversions back upon childhood? Returning for the moment to Emmy's case, it may be asked why, if her memory fused two temporally remote scenes into a single scene of seduction, it would not be just as plausible to say that she distributed in a temporal sequence the simultaneous events of a *single* childhood experience. Laplanche states, "Nothing prevents us from wondering whether the girl, on the very first occasion, had not gone into the store, moved by some sexual premonition. The separation, isolation and cleavage in memory would function to free the subject from guilt."[19]

Freud did not entertain this alternative explanation—his early conviction that a state of childhood innocence invariably preceded the "fall" would not permit it. Yet this interpretation is consistent with his claim that childhood memories are often distorted or censored by the author when he or she is not yet prepared to face the implications of past actions or desires. Having been confronted with repressed ideas that clearly were not straightforward recollections of patients' actual experiences, Freud proposed that fantasies must be an imaginary reworking of childhood experiences carried out in the interest of repression: "Fantasies are psychical facades constructed in order to bar the way to infantile memories. Fantasies at the same time serve the trend toward refining the memories, toward sublimating them."[20]

On the question of how to sift out the true from the counterfeit, Freud continued to use resistance as an index of the truthfulness of a patient's recollections. This method was of dubious value, however, since the same episode could be reasonably interpreted as either a painful overcoming of repressed memories or as the intensified labor of defense. Freud upheld his interpretation of Emmy's case as an example of a painful confrontation with her past, whereas Laplanche believes Freud had been deceived by yet another elaborate disguise, a fantasy designed to repress Emmy's desire to be seduced as a child. Hence, the same kind of argument made in defense of the reality of the seduction scene can be employed to refute it. Which interpretation we accept appears to depend on whose powers of storytelling we finding more convincing.

Apparently unconvinced by his own arguments for the existence of the seduction scene, in a letter written to Wilhelm Fliess in September 1897, Freud abruptly changed his position and confessed that he no longer believed in his "neurotica."[21] He offered several reasons for rejecting the seduction theory. One, to which I have just alluded, was that it seemed doubtful that treatment could overcome all resistance and retrieve the unalloyed truth about the patient's troubled past. Second, Freud grew frustrated at his inability to bring analysis to a resolution, an indication that he did not yet fully understand the etiology of psychoneuroses. Moreover, the implication that so many fathers were guilty of sexually abusing their children strained credulity. But what proved most important for the development of psychoanalysis was the realization that "there is no indication of reality in the unconscious, so that it is impossible to distinguish between truth and emotionally charged fiction [emphasis mine]."[22]

If the aim of psychoanalysis is to make the unconscious conscious, then it appears that the key to a science of neuroses is not an understanding of what objectively happened in the patient's past but an appreciation of how the patient's report and the analyst's narrative together fashion the intelligible fiction of the patient's story. The unconscious, in other words, effectively brackets the questions of veracity and objectivity. Its effects in the therapy hour would seem to be the sole concern of the analyst.

Freud's disillusionment with the seduction theory did not lead him to abandon his search for the truth about his patients, but it did force him to reevaluate the nature of fantasy and to formulate a new etiology which featured the concept of infantile sexuality. In the context of the seduction theory, fantasies had been viewed as a ploy to disguise infantile sexual memories for the purpose of repression. By appealing to the mechanism of deferred action, Freud had hoped to retrace traumatic events originating in early childhood. Now, however, patients' seduction stories were themselves recognized as fantasies that adults would invent in recounting their childhood. This seemed to imply that fantasies were, after all, retrospective constructions projected back from adulthood to early childhood.

Freud's reappraisal of neurotic fantasies obviously posed a serious threat to psychoanalysis. How could the analyst decide with certainty whether therapy achieved its avowed aim of anamnesis or merely elicited imaginary tales from patients? Apart from the question of whether a specific story generated in therapy warranted belief, what evidence demonstrated the capacity of memory to retrieve or represent scenes from the remote past? These questions were answered by situating the fantastic seduction stories of neurotics in a history not of events but of sexual impulses, fantasies and scenarios of fulfillment reaching back to infancy. Freud speculated in the course of self-analysis that infantile attraction of males to their mothers and jealousy of their fathers is a normal, universal phenomenon. In children susceptible to neuroses, these innate impulses would possess an abnormal degree of intensity. Rather than conceding that neuroses arose entirely from contemporary experience, Freud thus reverted to the idea of hereditary predisposition, now in the guise of the Oedipus complex. Unable to locate the primary trauma in a specifiable scene from childhood, Freud returned to the alternative of "sexual constitution" to supply an adequate explanation. If the reality of the historical origin proved to be a fiction, then he would invoke physiology for a scientific account of traumatic fictions: "Accidental influences derived from the experiences having thus receded into the background, the factors of constitution and heredity gained the upper hand once more; but there was this difference between my views and those prevailing in other quarters, that on my theory the 'sexual constitution' took the place of 'general neuropathic disposition.' "[23]

Although the severity of the impulse supplanted traumatic childhood experiences as the chief determinant, Freud did suggest that the genesis of psychoneuroses involves an interaction between less dramatic events and infantile impulses. Fantasy must draw its material from the fund of actual experience and it appeared plausible that a minor incident (e.g., the sight of one's mother nude) might be erotically embellished in the fantasy life of the child. Repressed fantasies, once uncovered and analyzed, still betrayed memories of actual childhood events, but these fantasies were no longer understood as defensive tactics aimed at screening or reworking painful memories. Quite the opposite, fantasies were now conceived as the gratification of impulses which had been repressed in childhood and reawakened in puberty. Instead of investigating the deferred memories of traumatic events, Freud now traced neurotic symptoms to infantile desires which had never been consummated save as deeds committed in the imagination. Guilt, he discovered, can be created by desires as well as by acts. The lesson of psychoanalysis was that the events which never happen control the ones that do. Freud made this point in more prosaic but no less perplexing terms.

> Influenced by Charcot's view of the traumatic origin of hysteria, one was readily inclined to accept as true and etiologically significant statements made by patients in which they ascribe their symptoms to . . . sexual experiences in the first years of childhood—to put it bluntly, to seduction. When this etiology broke down under the weight of its own improbability and contradiction in definitely ascertainable circumstances, the result was helpless bewilderment. Analysis had led me back to these infantile traumas by the right path, and yet they were not true. . . . But *if hysterical subjects trace their symptoms to traumas by the right path, then the new fact which emerges is precisely that they create such scenes in fantasy and this psychical reality must be taken into account alongside practical reality.* [Emphasis mine.][24]

Psychical and Practical Reality

The contrast of psychical with practical reality was prefigured by Freud's formulation in a letter to Fleiss, "Reality—wish fulfillment. It is from this pair of opposites that our mental life springs."[25] The concept of psychical reality initially denoted the unconscious wish and the fantasy associated with it but was later enlarged to include the regressive structure of the primary process—which has its locus in the unconscious—along with the dissimulating mechanisms of condensation and displacement.[26] Dreams, neuroses, and artistic works were cited as the chief examples of how fantasy constitutes a psychical realm with an autonomy and consistency equal in validity to its external counterpart. Yet if psychical reality gets its sense as illusion—as the distortion and derivative of (external) reality—precisely how can the psychical be a putative "reality" with a truth and dignity all its own? The ambiguity lies in the nature of fantasy as a domain that shades into both the real and the imaginary.

Freud's discovery of "psychical reality" was the outcome of a movement of thought in which the terms informing the polarities of inside/outside, constitution/event, and truth/fiction all were displaced in an effort to capture the "material itself." Retracing our steps, I noted earlier that Freud's turn to psychology was signaled by his rejection of a strictly anatomical conception of psychopathology. Meynert maintained that hysteria, or the overt behavior designated by that term, was a feigned illness, malingering by its so-called victims, for no internal lesion could be located which might produce the symptoms that had been observed. Following Charcot, Freud began according a role in symptom formation to both the internal events of the nervous system and the external circumstances of the patient's life. Despite references to heredity, physiological forces, and dynamic abnormalities, the precise nature of nonanatomical mechanisms or unobserved forces inferred from overt behavior still eluded Freud. Looking elsewhere for an answer, he loosened his discourse from its physiological moorings and conceptualized the work of repression as a psychological or ideogenic phenomenon. The most salient features of defense neuroses were subsequently ascribed to past scenes of conflict symbolized by neurotic symptoms.

The task of psychoanalysis became one of investigating traumatic memories separated or dissociated from the mainstream of psychic life. This development suggests that, although Freud abandoned anatomy, he was still concerned with locating the neurotic's source of distress in the resistance of memory to consciousness. The schema of deferred action, in which the trauma lost its character as a single substantial event of external origin, was meant to safeguard the seduction theory. However, its value for us consists in the model it provides for understanding the narrative structure of fantasy—something that became clear only long after the seduction theory had been abandoned.

Freud, we have seen, considered two alternatives to the failed seduction theory: fantasies of childhood as a retrospective construction performed by adults (Zurückphantasieren) and hereditary predisposition. Having chosen the latter, Freud returned to biological realism, but his physiology now lacked the rich structural implications of his study of aphasia and the role of sexuality in the significations of deferred action. The theory of infantile sexuality enabled Freud to attribute "psychical reality" to the spontaneous appearance of endogenous sexuality in childhood and its evolution according to fixed stages of libidinal development. Fantasy, in this view, is a kind of epiphenomenon or by-product of purely biological tendencies.

This turn to biology led Freud out of his impasse but only at the expense of ignoring, at least temporarily, important epistemological questions regarding those polarities which defined the field of psychoanalytic inquiry: recollection/reconstruction, practical reality / psychical reality, text/event, desire for truth / resistance to truth. As Laplanche and Leclaire state, "Paradoxically, at the moment that fantasy emerged as the fundamental object of psychoanalysis, its distinctive character was obscured by the emphasis on infantile sexuality."[27] Once the relevant entity was reformulated as an instinctual wish, Freud could readily discern the influence of age upon the aim and object of desire. This set the stage for the discovery of regularities in psychosexual development which, in turn, inspired him to hunt for the disguised wishes that had eluded him earlier. Since unconscious or repressed wishes are volitional ideas split off from consciousness, it could be argued that the principles of anatomy (locality) and physiology (force) persisted in

Freud's mature psychology, influencing the form if not the content of psychoanalytic inquiry.

This picture of psychoanalysis, in which "traumatic fictions" are psychic events plotted along the course of psychosexual development, fails to appreciate how the premise of an epistemological realism was ultimately challenged by Freud's inquiry into the structure and origin of fantasy. Despite his renewed emphasis on heredity and endogenous sexuality, the psychic realm would not fall neatly into the physiological or historical series of events that belonged to his earlier etiological equations.

The context for my reassessment of Freud's later views of mental life—and mental fictions—is the case history. The striking resemblance of Freud's case histories to fictional narratives invited the question whether the psychological explanation of neuroses was not itself a fiction. Freud, we have seen, acknowledged that both imaginative works and case histories derived their explanatory power from the concordance of beginnings, middles, and endings which satisfied the analyst's/author's appetite for closure or internal coherence. If narrative structure alone compels our acceptance of a case history, on what grounds can it be said that the origins of neuroses recovered by Freud occurred in the manner described in analysis and recorded in the written summary of the case? Freud's statement that traumas are fictions insinuates the imaginary into the heart of psychoanalysis. The so-called referents of his narratives are actions not performed but fantasized. This move appears to have undermined his earlier appeal to empirically verified scenes as justification of his stories. The seduction theory had deceived Freud in much the same way that his patients had been seduced by their fictions. In order to defend the integrity of psychoanalysis, he would have to steer a middle course between veridical memory and the imaginary understood as illusion. Psychical reality has all of the consistency and efficacy of the real without, however, being verifiable in "external" experience. If the realm of fantasy is not, at bottom, amenable to biological explanation, then it remains to be seen how the terms "psychical" and "reality" can be merged. The domain of psychoanalysis is likewise open to question: how are science and fiction brought into its compass?

Tales of the Wolf Man: The Case Study Method

In order to elucidate the distinction between practical and psychical reality, to see how they stand "alongside" one another, I wish to examine Freud's case history of the Wolf Man, an infantile neurosis which was reported and analyzed fifteen years after its termination as part of a more complete analysis of an adult neurosis. The case represents Freud's mature views on the etiology of neuroses, particularly the influence of sexual desire and fantasy at all stages of libidinal development. In addition to detailing the effects of infantile sexuality of the neurotic imagination, the case displays brilliantly Freud's skills of psychoanalytic detection. The case was a fitting test of his clinical technique, not only because of the patient's present distance from the childhood neurosis, but also because of the resistance along the way which disguised and displaced the analyst's quarry. In Freud's words, "I will once more recall that our therapeutic work was concerned with a subsequent and recent neurotic illness, and that light could be thrown upon the earlier problems when the course of the analysis led away for a time from the present, and forced us to make a detour through the pre-historic period of childhood."[28] In his dual role as detective and archaeologist, Freud probed the secrets of "pre-historic" childhood to solve the mystery of the adult patient's illness. The complexity of his method stemmed from the difficult task of composing a narrative (historical) account of the patient's etiology with a structural (archaeological) topography of the psyche's primitive level of organization. These competing explanatory demands were reflected in expository problems that plagued Freud as he set out to report the case: "I am unable to give either a purely historical or a purely thematic account of my patient's illness; I can write a history neither of the treatment nor of the illness, but I shall find myself obliged to combine the two methods of presentation."[29]

If the difficulties involved in presenting a unified, linear plot to the reader were tied to the demands of the method, the latter, in turn, sprang from the peculiar nature of the material under investigation. Problems of exposition and explanation were due specifically to the limitations encountered in mapping a multidimensional phenomenon on a two-dimensional plane:

> So it was that his mental life impressed one in much the same way as the religion of ancient Egypt, which is unintelligible to us because it preserves the earlier stages of its development side to side with the end products, retains the most ancient gods and their significations, along with the most modern ones, and thus, as it were, spreads out upon a two-dimensional surface what other instances show us in the solid.[30]

The order of presentation ("two-dimensional plane") in the published case history must somehow integrate material drawn from the story of the infantile neurosis, the etiological chain of events which precipitated the neurosis, and the story of past events during the analysis and treatment. Each of these three stories needed reshaping to fit the significant plot of the finished narrative known as "From the History of an Infantile Neurosis." Freud's preliminary remarks concerning the composition of the case were not accidental, then, to the history being told. The importance of this point will become evident as we follow Freud's labyrinthine path to the Wolf Man's prehistory and the origins of his childhood neurosis.

The history of the illness opens with the patient's recollections of childhood. As a small boy, he was looked after by his loving nurse, an illiterate woman of peasant birth. He returned his Nanya's affection and was generally a good-natured, quiet boy. But in the summer of his fourth year, when his parents returned from their holiday, they found him changed. He became violent and irritable and later developed symptoms of an animal phobia and obsessive piety.

The Wolf Man recounted in analysis a recurring childhood dream which Freud analyzed in order to reach an understanding of the boy's sudden change in character. The dreams all contained sexually aggressive actions committed by the Wolf Man toward his older sister, actions which Freud interpreted as fantasies that disguised the memory of another scene, a real event in the patient's past. Having been initiated into sexual practices by his sister, the Wolf Man, Freud claimed, sought through his dream to suppress the memory of an event which offended his masculine self-esteem. In Freud's words, the dream, which substituted aggressiveness for the patient's passive role in the seduction, served the purpose of defense "by putting an imaginary and desirable converse in the place of the historical truth. . . . The fantasies corresponded exactly to the legends by means of which a nation that has been great and proud tries to conceal the failure of its beginnings."[31]

We would expect Freud to exercise caution in his dream interpretation after being deceived earlier in his career by seduction stories that proved to be fictions. Yet despite having withdrawn belief in the truth of his patients' reports, he now reinstated the seduction theory by pronouncing the content of the dream a fantasy and its transposition a historical fact. Sweeping past doubts aside, Freud did not entertain the alternative hypothesis that the seduction, itself the referent of the dream, might refer obliquely to an even earlier incident in the child's past.

Two kinds of evidence were offered to support his interpretation: one was empirical, the other (con)textual in nature. The reality of the seduction was empirically substantiated by the testimony of a cousin, who recalled that the Wolf Man's sister had been sexually precocious as a child. Freud drew textual evidence for the seduction scene from the patient's memories and associations, including the recollection of seeing his sister urinating from her "wound" and of hearing a story in which a wolf lost its "tail." These and other elements from the patient's report supplied the material for Freud's thematic construction of castration. Unlike the cousin's "eyewitness" account, no single element of the patient's report referred directly to the seduction scene. Instead, the patient's allusions to phallic imagery—his description of candysticks as "chopped snakes" is another example—collectively formed a narrative context, the thematic construction in and through which each element of the report gained its significance and explanatory power. Analysis depended on integrating the elements into an interpretive whole and then showing how that theme found expression in the behavior or symbolic action of the patient. The reality of the seduction scene seemed plausible—if not certain—because it enabled Freud to present a complete, coherent explanation of the illness as a response to the threat of castration by the patient's sister.

This explanation depended, of course, on an elaborate theory of sexual organization without which the theme of a castration complex could be neither detected nor understood. The sexual etiology traced neurotic maladies to arrests or regressions of sexual aims, and these arrests, in turn, were said to express the conflict between the libido and impediments hindering its free gratification. Having been sexually awakened by his sister, the boy tried to win his beloved Nanya by openly masturbating in her presence. He was rebuffed for his assertion of masculinity and warned that boys who do such things get a "wound" in that place. When the boy stopped masturbating under the threat of castration, "his sexual life, which was beginning to come under the sway of his genital zone, gave way before an external obstacle and was thrown back by its influence into an earlier phase of pregenital organization."[32] His sexual life now took on an anal-sadistic character manifested in the verbal abuse of his nursemaid and the torture of small animals. Directed toward himself, his outward hostility was converted into masochistic behavior. After being refused by his Nanya, the boy pursued his father "in an attempt to renew his first and most primitive object choice which, in conformity with a small child's narcissism, had taken place along the path of identification."[33] The boy's fits of rage on the return of his parents were meant to force beatings from his father which would satisfy his desire to be seduced and the need to alleviate his sense of guilt.

The connecting threads of Freud's construction again wove a

vivid picture of the seduction of the Wolf Man by his sister, since it was the effect of this incident that must have motivated his unruly behavior. The traumatic power of this premature sexual experience set the young boy on a path that led from his sister to his nursemaid and from Nanya to his father. At the same time, his passive attitude toward women as the victim of his sister's advance extended to his attitude toward men as well: "His father was now his object choice once more in conformity with a higher stage of development; identification was replaced by his object choice while the transformation of his active attitude into a passive one was the consequence and the record of the seduction which had occurred meanwhile."[34]

Tales of the Wolf Man: The Search for Origins

We have seen how confirmation of the traumatic origin by correspondence between event and veridical memory operated alongside confirmation by the coherence of the analyst's constructed narrative. As Jonathan Culler has observed, empirical and textual arguments belonged to the double logic of Freud's case histories.[35] As a vehicle of empirical inquiry, the narrative faithfully documented preexisting events uncovered by analysis. At the same time, Freud's textual reconstruction provided the more compelling defense of the seduction scene by showing how it was necessitated by the thematic structure of castration anxiety. Both principles were satisfied in Freud's detection of the seduction scene. However, the analysis was not yet complete—pieces were still missing from the puzzle, the origins of the patient's illness still awaited "discovery."

The phase of unruly and perverse behavior that immediately followed the patient's seduction scene was not accompanied by neurotic symptoms. Only after a traumatic event at age four did a longer phase of neurotic symptoms ensue. The event that mediated between the origin of the illness and its symptomatic effects was not an external trauma but a wolf dream from which the boy awoke in a fit of anxiety. Freud was convinced that the dream was positioned as the decisive event in the history of the illness, an event that produced by deferred action—now operating entirely within childhood—a neurotic reaction to both the seduction scene which had occurred six months earlier and to a primal scene in which he had witnessed his parents copulating *a tergo* two and a half years earlier.

Although story and plot are relative terms—"what happened" sometimes refers to the procedure for investigating or composing the story—the justification of a nonfictional narrative or story demands that the distinction be preserved. "The Tale of Many Tongues" raised the general question of authorial bias in presenting a plot that falsifies the events it seeks to represent. If what happened is ultimately reducible to how it is rendered by the narrator, then we lose any means of determining the fidelity of any narrative to its presumed subject matter. The gap between them—as between a hypothesis and its data— is the space of verification.

The closing of this gap is precisely the problem posed by the wolf dream. Considered as an experience that exerted a powerful influence over the course of the patient's illness, the dream belonged to the linear sequence of events ("what happened") that lay outside and behind Freud's text. Yet the dream also functioned as a primary text or plot whose associations (from the patient) and interpretation (from the analyst) ultimately shaped Freud's understanding of the nature and order of events constituting the etiology (story) of the illness. The dream, in other words, functioned both as a historical document that explained the analysand's remote past and as a causally significant incident within the chain of events constituting his neurotic etiology. Peter Brooks makes this point succinctly when he writes, "The dream is a text which both explains and alters the reality to which it refers."[36]

Freud's puzzlement at why the specific symptoms of an animal phobia and obsessive piety would afflict his patient as a child moved him to trace the symptoms back to an instigating scene predating the seduction. The interpretation of the wolf dream, the sole access to the patient's prehistory, proceeded from the several fragments of the patient's report. Although the dream was restaged at the beginning of analysis, it was not fully elucidated until four years later.

Dream fragments, like symptoms, were regarded as associative structures which both reveal and conceal their intended meaning. The sense or coherence of the thematic material suggested by the dream and the conscious associations of the patient emerged only after all the dream elements had been narrativized—unraveled and reordered—into a plausible sequence of events. An adequate understanding of the dream—considered as both an event in the course of the illness and the narrative rendering of the illness—ultimately required, in Freud's view, the discovery of the origin as the scene which lay concealed behind the dream, at its source.[37] After undoing the "false connections" of displacement and condensation, Freud arranged the dream elements in a thematic representation of the primal scene he was seeking:

> What sprang into activity that night out of the chaos of the dreamer's unconscious memory-traces was the picture of the copulation between his parents, copulation in circumstances which were not entirely usual and were especially favorable for observation. It gradually became possible to find satisfactory answers to all the questions that arose in connection with this scene; for in the course of the treatment, the first dream returned in innumerable variations and new editions, in connection with which the analysis produced the information that was required.[38]

Freud's confidence that the reconstructed primal scene fully explained the wolf dream was underscored by his appeal to "memory-traces," an indelible historical record which somehow retained the scene's content and significance, making both available to the analyst for direct inspection. But a closer look at how Freud actually proceeded reveals an ambiguous, unstable relationship between text and event. The real scene allegedly preceded the dream in time as its cause, but Freud's interpretation was not constructed from the directly remembered or indirectly confirmed event standing outside the narrative of the analysand (report) or the analyst (edited report). Instead, the scene was itself fashioned solely from the semantic elements of the dream. Nevertheless, Freud insisted that reconstruction by the analyst is "absolutely equivalent to recollection." Dreaming, he continued, "is actually another kind of remembering, though one that is subject to the conditions that rule at night and to the laws of dream-formation. It is the recurrence in dreams that I regard as the explanation of the fact that the patients themselves gradually acquire a profound conviction which is in no respect inferior to one based on recollection."[39]

Although the dream allegedly substituted pictorial symbols for conscious memory of the traumatic scene, Freud's interpretation failed to trigger the shock of recognition or anamnesis that characterized his other success stories. Yet no question was raised whether some of the material eventually "recovered" from the patient's repressed unconscious may have been artifacts of the analyst's suggested interpretation. Instead, after urging provisional acceptance of the reality of the primal scene, the "sense of reality" being his only major argument for belief, Freud proceeded to put all the dream elements and the history of the illness into place.

This patterning of dream elements into a coherent text demanded the primal scene for its completion. Without the reconstructed origin, the dream would remain unintelligible; and once the origin was posited, no other interpretation seemed possible. An illustration of Freud's procedure should suffice to show how "internal necessity" guided his reconstruction of both the dream and the illness. The analysis concentrated on several dream elements: windows opening; the immobility of wolves; walnut trees by the window; and wolves in the trees. Freud maintained that by transposition with the attentive wolves in the dream, the eyes of the patient, not the window, opened and saw something. The patient was looking instead of being looked at, and what he saw was not stillness but violent motion. The walnut tree was an obvious association with a Christmas tree, a conclusion reinforced by the patient's recollection that he had the dream shortly before Christmas and in expectation of the holiday. The dream therefore expressed the wish for "gifts" in anticipation of both Christmas and his approaching fourth birthday. However, the gifts in the Christmas tree were transformed into frightening wolves. The image of the wolves was drawn from two fairy tales, one in which a wolf lost its tail, an obvious allusion to castration.

Freud speculated that the posture of the wolf in the fairy tale

"The Wolf and the Seven Little Goats" might have reminded the
patient of his father during the reconstructed primal scene. The
picture became the point of departure for further manifestations of anxiety as the repudiation of the wish for gifts—sexual
satisfaction—which was the motive for the Wolf Man's dream.
The fear of being eaten by the wolf betrayed the child's concern
that if his wish to copulate with his father were fulfilled, he
would suffer the same fate as his mother. In other words, if he
were sexually satisfied in the same fashion, he, too, would lose
his "tail" and suffer a "wound" in its place. Once the boy's passive attitude toward his father succumbed to repression, the
fear of his father surfaced in the shape of a wolf phobia. His
mother, of course, assumed the role of the castrated wolf, and
the father was represented by the wolf that mounted her. The
dream thus represented the boy's identification with his castrated mother and rebellion against his father. His masculinity
protested against being castrated like his mother in order to be
sexually satisfied by his father.

Again, each of the dream elements was made intelligible by
showing how it derived from the primal scene, but the primal
scene was itself a construction from the elements of the dream
report. The origin/cause was exhibited in a cluster of associations, each term gaining meaning from other terms in the associative structure rather than from its direct correspondence to
an extra-mental referent. Even though the primal scene issued
from the dream's internal logic of signification, Freud argued
that the event must have occurred as the origin and cause of the
later neurosis. "I must therefore," he concluded, "be left at this
(I can see no other possibility): Either the analysis based on the
neurosis in his childhood is all a piece of nonsense from start to
finish, or else everything took place just as I have described it
here."[40]

Although there is no indication of (external) reality in the
unconscious, psychoanalysis seemed eminently capable of
distinguishing between truth and emotionally charged fiction.
Because his interpretation met the criteria for a well-formed
narrative—adequacy, completeness, coherence—Freud was
convinced that the primal scene must have occurred. Culler

suggests that Freud was guilty of the fallacy of bifurcation. If the scene were not a real event, would we be justified in dismissing his narrative as nonsense? Must a meaningful, instructive narrative square with empirically verifiable events, or is it also possible that the reconstruction of the primal scene was a meaningful, overdetermined fiction?[41]

Freud did not entertain this further possibility until four years after the completion of his study. In 1918 he resumed discussion of the wolf dream in what he called a "supplementation and rectification" of his original, and seemingly definitive, explanation. In an abrupt reversal, not unlike his sudden change of heart concerning the reality of childhood seductions, he now proposed that the primal scene was not a real event at all but itself a construction, a transference from, say, a scene of copulating dogs to his parents which produced at age four a fantasy of witnessing at age one and a half a scene of parental copulation. Freud offered as evidence of this scenario the same structural coherence that had previously convinced him that the primal scene was a real event: "The scene which was to be made up had to fulfill certain conditions which, in consequence of the circumstances of the dreamer's life, could only be found in precisely the early period; such, for instance, was the condition that he should be in his parents' bedroom."[42]

In the text of the case history the earlier interpretation of the scene as actual event "stands alongside" the later, bracketed interpretation of the scene as fantasy. Rather than suppressing or reediting the original version, Freud now reluctantly conceded that even if the primal scene were not an (external) event, its (internal) construction in fantasy might generate the same case history. As David Carroll has noted, whether the reality of the primal scene is simple or multiple, substantial or fantastic, does not affect the development of the structure of fantasies which constitutes the analysand's neurosis.[43] Rather than insisting that textual interpretation must match a real, observable event, Freud now acknowledged the alternative that eluded him earlier. His narrative suggests, in Peter Brooks's words, "another kind of referentiality, in that all tales may lead back not so much to events but to other tales, to man as a structure of fictions that he tells about himself."[44] This peculiar kind of reference, in which memory find its "object" not in corresponding events but in other significations, does not respect the sharp conceptual distinction between empirical certainty and illusory fiction. If the primal scene is a fantasy, the construction is no less powerful precisely because the analysand construes the origin as a verifiable event. At the same time, if the analyst regards the scene as an empirical "event," the origin possesses causal efficacy only because it is required by the analysand's structure of signification.[45] As Freud finally admitted, regardless of which version we embrace, the unfolding story of the neurosis and its treatment remains identical: "I should myself be glad to know whether the primal scene in my present patient's case was a fantasy or a real experience; but, taking other similar cases into account, I must admit that the answer to this question is not in fact a matter of very great importance."[46]

In his search for evidence to support a particular interpretation, Freud had shown a regressive tendency toward the origin, the foundation upon which the conceptual edifice of the analyst's story would rest. Although the Wolf Man case history continued this search for a founding event—"the material itself"—it forced Freud radically to question the status of the origin as the first in a sequence of events occurring outside and prior to their narrative reconstruction.

Psychical reality now appears not as a "subjective" species of event, the internal counterpart of what Freud called practical reality, but as a place of undecidability, in which the dichotomies between actual scene and fantasy, sick patient and omniscient analyst/narrator, can no longer be sharply drawn. Indeed, it can be said that the case history is itself a blurred genre, a composition which does not fall squarely within the bounds of fictional storytelling or nonfictional discourse. Freud did not abdicate his responsibility for distinguishing truth from fiction, but his attempt to sort them out only deepened the epistemological dilemma of psychoanalysis as he deferred the origins of the Wolf Man's illness to the mythical beginnings of the race.

Freud's impatience with ambiguities surrounding the nature

of the primal scene—with the lack of narrative closure—moved him to speculate that what occurred as fantasy in the child must have had its source in the distant origins of the species: "[The child] fills in gaps in individual truth with prehistoric truth; he replaces occurrences in his own life by occurrences in the life of his ancestors."[47] If the individual plot has no clear beginning, then it must be placed within a collective history, the masterplot sketched in *Totem and Taboo* (1912–13).

Having accepted Darwin's thesis that primitive man gathered in small hordes tyrannically ruled by a patriarchal figure, Freud conjectured that the brothers in the primal horde committed "a memorable and criminal deed," the slaying of the despotic father, in order to gain an equitable distribution of the erotic goods. The act of parricide was followed by pangs of remorse and guilt, which lay behind all social organization, religion, and morality. Guilt, in other words, was the motive force behind the creation of taboos against the twin crimes of parricide and incest. The primal drama is our inheritance, passed from generation to generation through the medium of memory traces. Because modern man repeats the wish, if not the actual deed, the guilt that attends the desire to commit the crime asserts the ancient claim of memory. Apologists for Freud point out that the scenario is defensible not as empirical anthropology but as a dramatization of the social contract which recognized the irremediable antagonism between individual impulses and societal norms. If guilt can be created by desires as well as acts, it makes no difference whether the prehistoric scene ever took place. In *Totem and Taboo* Freud did entertain the possibility that remorse may have been provoked by the sons' fantasy of parricide; yet the pattern of inquiry present in the Wolf Man case history repeated itself: "It must be confessed that the distinction which may seem fundamental to other people does not in our judgment affect the heart of the matter."[48] Once again, as Culler reminds us, regardless of whether the origin is construed as an empirical event or as a signification, the configuration of desire captured in the narrative remains the same. Even so, Freud's own desire for the truth forced him to choose one perspective over the other: "Primitive man was uninhibited. . . . I think in the case before us it may be assumed that 'in the beginning was the Deed.' "[49]

Freud would later realize that the desire to remember beginnings is rivaled by psychic resistance, the desire to forget. The interminable movement of interpretation, as both Ricoeur and Lacan have noted, is not driven by the plenitude of memory but by its insufficiency or lack. Although the founding event eluded Freud, the origin functioned simultaneously as the impetus to narrative and its destination, whether produced in the guise of a fantasy, a transference, a lost or absent origin which prolongs the search.[50] The text of analysis and the nature of the patient's illness both can be characterized in these terms. "Genuine desire," Frederic Jameson writes, "is a consent to incompleteness and to the repetition of desire in time, whereas the disorders of desire result from an attempt to keep alive the delusion and fiction of ultimate satisfaction."[51] Psychoanalysis, considered as both a literary form and epistemological commitment, desired nothing more—was obsessed with nothing less—than completeness. I have already remarked that the case history owes its narrative form to the familiar plot of the detective story. In the detective story, the crime has already occurred outside the narrative. The story opens with the discovery of the corpse and unfolds as the effort to discover something that happened long ago. Similarly, Freud's analysis and its written record as a case history would begin in medias res, long after the primal scene produced its symptomatic effects. Faced with scattered clues in the patient's report, the analyst eventually would discover the decisive event concealed behind the illness. The case history, like the detective story, ends—after a long detour and many blind alleys—when all the significant traumatic events predating the story's beginning have been traced to their origin. The case history thus demonstrated positivistic confidence that the problem could be clearly defined, evidence gathered, and a solution achieved by skillfully applying the appropriate method.

The Wolf Man case history, by vividly documenting the unfulfilled search for an ending and a solution, dramatizes the modern experience of uncertainty and anxiety which makes

Freud's stories structures of undecidability. As I set out to recount the case study, I emphasized that Freud's inability to synthesize historical (sequential) and thematic (structural) dimensions was not due to his failings as a writer but to the recalcitrance of the material itself. The material was distributed between the causal sequence of events that led to the neurosis and the narrative reconstruction of the illness in the therapy hour. Because Freud was not content to locate the origin of the symptoms *either* "outside" the narrative as an external event or "within" the patient's imagination as a "psychical" one, the case study ends without resolving questions concerning the truth or fiction of the primal scene. Despite our early education in "reality testing," we can no longer sharply distinguish between the literal and the figurative, between psychological events and their narrative construction.

If the unconscious occupies the zone *between* analyst and analysand, then it was perhaps best described by Merleau-Ponty as "the index of an enigma."[52] I have tried to show that the unconscious does not lurk somewhere in the shadows of the mind but surfaces in the struggle to make sense. Both the obsessive quality of the analysis and the incompleteness of the narrative mirror the pathology of the patient who cannot integrate the details of his or her life into a believable, unified story. Narrative insufficiency and neurotic anxiety are diagnostic categories that apply not merely to the patient who seeks a cure but to the interminable—indeed incurable—condition of psychoanalytic inquiry as well. Psychoanalysis, in order to probe the unconscious, must be implicated in the workings of desire, the displacements and misrecognitions that menace those who attempt to reclaim as well as to forget the past.

4

History and Historicality in Psychoanalysis

In the opening paragraphs of *The Use and Abuse of History,* Nietzsche told the parable of an unhappy man who sought the counsel of a contented beast: " 'Why do you look at me and not speak of your happiness?' The beast wants to answer, 'Because I always forget what I wished to say,' but he forgets the answer, too; and man is left to wonder."[1] The irony is plain: the search after happiness is precisely the anxious, unhappy state from which humankind unknowingly seeks escape.

Endowed with a sense of the passage of time, people are uniquely capable of interrogating their origins and of envisaging a future. Unlike the beast of the field, whose life is a fixed repertoire, humans experience succession, delight in difference, and seek change as they control the course of their life. If temporal awareness singles humans out as a gifted species, then why do they envy the beast? The desire to improve their life lead them to contemplate the source of their unhappiness; yet it is precisely the capacity for memory that has caused them anguish. In Nietzsche's words, man is "an imperfect tense striving vainly to become a present."[2] The human impulse to live fully and immediately in the present is frustrated by that part of life experienced as finished, determined, resistant to change. Man may rush forward to disown or shake off his past, but "however far and fast he runs, that chain runs with him."[3] The

114

human animal, unable to live in a happy blindness between the walls of past and future, is portrayed as the true beast of burden who bears the "great and continually increasing weight of the past . . . pressing down and bowing his shoulders."[4]

It appears that humans can be relieved of their burden only when they learn to imitate the beast, whose happiness is the absence of speech and memory. But this is an unsatisfactory solution, since human forgetfulness bears no resemblance to animal oblivion. Forgetfulness implies the prior ability to remember—something lacking in the beast. When humans willfully forget the past, history is not abolished but conserved and augumented in importance as well. Both Nietzsche and Freud have taught us that the denial of personal antecedents results in destructive, life-defeating forms of memory that may be described as "abuses" of history.

How, then, should we regard the past in order not to be dominated by it? Memory and speech may be the very instruments of reflection which make us human and other species merely *alogos*, but the predominance of memory—its persistence in the present—all too often robs life of forgetfulness, the unhistorical condition which makes creativity possible. The challenge articulated by Nietzsche is to determine how humans as historical creatures can overcome their neurosis in the peculiarly human dialectic of remembering and forgetting. Psychoanalysis dramatizes Nietzsche's challenge through its interpretation of instinctual conflict. The "beast," having insinuated itself into the soul of humankind as its instinctual core, is now interrogated and forced to speak.

Nietzsche's reflections on history showed how attitudes toward the past may be either beneficial or inimical to life. A thoroughgoing Freudian, he understood all historical inquiry—his own included—in terms of its psychological motivation. Despite its pretensions to objectivity, the Prussian school led by Leopold von Ranke was also said to harbor a bias. The ideal of reconstructing the past "as it really was" (*wie es eigentlich gewesen ist*) betrayed, in Nietzsche's eyes, a dubious justification for conservatism. The dispassionate chronicling of "facts" was regarded with suspicion because it dulls people's capacity for evaluation and criticism. Objectivity, in other words, is not desirable, let alone attainable. In Nietzsche's view, an overdose of history is debilitating and engenders vacillation where action is required.

Freud, if we reverse the relationship, was a qualified Nietzschian. As a therapist he saw clearly that recollection could serve as a tool to excavate the buried past and to condemn its pernicious influence in the symptomatology of the analysand. Yet in his capacity as a scientist, Freud was faced with a different kind of task. If the problem in treatment was to liberate his patients from the effects of an overpreserved past, his obligation as a scientist was to retrieve and chronicle distant scenes of trauma—real or imagined—that had been distorted by the passage of time and by the analysand's defensive maneuvers. Although Freud finally admitted that there are no innocent biographical facts, we generally find in psychoanalysis a neat division between history as symptom/cure and history as explanatory method. In the first instance, the closeness, indeed tyranny, of the past was Freud's chief obstacle to success; in the second, it was precisely the remoteness of an individual's or culture's prehistory that tested the explanatory powers of psychoanalysis. Therapy, as a mode of self-understanding, opens the distance between past and present, whereas psychoanalytic explanation closes it.

I am not suggesting that we should collapse the epistemological and therapeutic dimensions of psychoanalysis so that all explanation becomes the function of instinct, wish, or will to power. Nevertheless, Nietzsche's analysis brings into relief an intention in Freud's writings that is easily overlooked. Quite independently of the problem of historical explanation is the more fundamental issue of how time and history are constitutive—and regulative—of human lives. What is distinctive about humankind is that "this entity is not temporal because it stands in history but . . . on the contrary, it exists historically and can so exist in the very basis of its being."[5]

This statement was made not by Nietzsche but by Heidegger and, together with Nietzsche's parable, it serves to shift the emphasis of this book from questions within historiography to questions concerning the conditions underlying any historical inquiry into that measurable region of human experience that we call the past. The idea of historicality (*Geschichtlichkeit*) pervades *Being and Time* but is systematically developed in part 2 of that work as that feature of man's ontological constitution which makes history possible, both as science (*Historie*) and as the event or theme of historical inquiry (*Geschichte*).[6]

Freud never thematized, as did Heidegger, the nature of historicality. The case studies exhibited connections between temporality and narrative, but the conditions or principles of historical existence were never addressed explicitly in his theoretical writings. However, I do think the theory of instincts, "Beyond the Pleasure Principle" in particular, can be better understood in light of Heidegger's hermeneutical inquiry than the natural sciences to which Freud turned for support of his models of the mind.

Against the standard view of metapsychology as the return of repressed positivism, I intend to show that beneath the "manifest content" of Freud's metapsychology is a metabiography, that is, the heuristic model of the psyche as a textual economy—the "binding" of textual or interpretive "energies." After reviewing two divergent interpretations of the psychoanalytic conception of history, I will introduce Peter Brooks's unusual treatment of "Beyond the Pleasure Principle" as a dynamic model for the comprehension of plots.[7] Drawing from Brooks's essay, I intend to show how the metapsychology is indispensable for an understanding of how the dynamics of memory and narrative operate in case histories and the stories that give shape to all human lives. Finally, I will indicate how Freud and Heidegger both elucidate the concept of historicality through a comparison of the death instinct [*Thanatos*] with the phenomenon of being-towards-death [*Sein-zum-Tode*] set out in *Being and Time*.

Brown and Rieff: Two Views of Psychoanalysis and History

In his work on Freud, *Life against Death*, Norman O. Brown traces Nietzsche's connection between neurosis and history by arguing that repression introduces the human experience of time. Under the condition of repression, humans establish a fixation to the past that alienates them from the present and commits them to seek gratification of their infantile wishes in the future: "The discontented animal," Brown asserts, "is the neurotic animal, the animal with desires given in nature which cannot be satisfied by culture."[8] If time is a function of repression, then the cure for neurosis must be found in the unification of the ego and id, which would release people from the bonds of time. In his own words, "If historical consciousness is finally transformed into psychoanalytical consciousness, the grip of the dead hand of the past would be loosened, and man would be ready to live instead of making history, to enjoy instead of paying back old scores and debts, and to enter that state of Being which is the goal of his becoming."[9]

After crediting Freud with a profound diagnosis of the "disease called man," Brown asks for nothing less from psychoanalysis than a transformation of human nature. The lesson we find in Freud's writings is one of humility. From Copernicus humankind has learned that the human world is not the center or purpose of the universe; from Darwin, that humans are members of the animal kingdom. Freud struck yet a third blow at people's narcissism by reminding us that the ego is not the master in its own house.[10] If, from a psychoanalytic perspective, repressed but immutable drives sustain the spectacle of history, then the illusion of progress is itself a feature of humankind's Faustian character. Indeed, Freud cautioned that the claims of reason to progress or cure may actually be the work of instinctual renunciation:

> An untiring impulsion toward perfection can easily be understood as a result of the instinctual repression upon which is based all that is most precious in human civilization. The repressed instincts never cease to strive for complete satisfaction. No substitutive or reaction formations and sublimations will suffice to remove the instincts' persisting tension.[11]

This passage does not refer specifically to the therapy hour but to the wider domain of cultural aspiration and achievement.

Yet any activity that appears to be an agent of change or prog-ress may betray the persistence of deflected and conservative instinctual aims. Therapy, of course, seeks to deepen the histor-ical consciousness of the individual, thereby enabling the anal-ysand to substitute reflection upon the past for its blind re-enactment. But by defining humankind as the organization or irremediable conflict between infantile wishes and cultural prohibitions, Freud has arguably made contemporaneity as a therapeutic ideal unattainable.

Brown concedes that the predominance of pain over plea-sure, frustration over satisfaction, and conflict over reconcilia-tion all issue from an intellectual realism which refused to ac-cept any cheap or easy solutions. However, he goes on to say that if Freud's instinctual dualism were to become an in-stinctual dialectic, humans might awaken from history as from a nightmare and enter the "Sabbath of Eternity."[12] Instinctual ambivalence is an immutable truth, argues Brown, only if we accept the idea that conflict between forces is inherent in organic life. If psychoanalysis is to keep open the possibility of therapy, it must find a way to avoid Freud's metaphysical vision of all life being sick with struggle. Man, Nietzsche proposed, is distinguished from animals by the privilege of being sick. If there is an essential connection between being sick and being civilized, instinctual ambivalence must be a *human* prerog-ative.

By restricting instinctual conflict to the human species, Brown finds an escape from neurosis. Humankind separates opposites (love/hate; life/death) out of the state of undifferenti-ated unity present in other species. Dualism leads to thera-peutic pessimism because it results in the representation of conflict not as human alienation but as biological necessity. Brown again: "Dualism prevents us from positing any break with nature and consequently precludes the notion of return to nature; and since the failure to posit a break with nature entails the necessity of projecting man's sickness into nature, a 'return' to nature would not be a return to health."[13]

Brown's romantic vision plots history as a departure from a condition of undifferentiated unity, an intermediate period in which the powers of humans are developed though differentiation and antagonism, and a final—not yet achieved—return to a unity on a higher level of harmony. The reunification of life and death can be envisioned only as the end of the historical process, as the abolition of history and reunification with nature.

Philip Rieff diverges sharply from Brown in seeing psychoanalysis as essentially ahistorical in method and pessimistic in mood.[14] In previous chapters, I have surveyed the primitive—primary process, primal scenes, primal fantasies—in mental life. Rieff's study traces psychoanalytic connections between the primitive and the sick or abnormal by showing how Freud applied the conceptual tools of the prototype and analogy to the psychology of society and the individual. Prototypal events, whether located in the mythical past (e.g., the slaying of the patriarch) or in the prehistory of childhood (e.g., the Wolf Man witnessing his copulating parents), are determinative of the entire developmental history that follows: "The experiences of the first five years of childhood exert a decisive influence on our life . . . and resist all efforts of modern civilization to modify them."[15]

As the locus of regression, the dream revives the most primitive and powerful wishes of childhood as well as the child's hallucinatory method of satisfaction. At the same time, the dream reveals behind the individual's childhood vestiges of the remote phylogenetic past. By means of analogy, Freud extended anthropological ideas about the "irrational" behavior of "primitives" to the behavior of neurotics and children. "In the mental life of children today," he wrote, "we can still detect the same archaic factors which were once dominant generally in the primaeval days of human civilization."[16] The mental disorders of neurotics are accordingly understood as remnants of the archetypal Oedipal drama enacted in early stages of human evolution.

Two shapes of time organized history for Freud: the line of unilinear progress and the circle of repetition. As a residue of his Enlightenment optimism, Freud proposed an evolutionary scheme which paralleled individual libidinal development to Comte's positivistic stages of history: animism corresponds to narcissim, religion to parental object choice, and science to the mature renunciation of the pleasure principle and adjustment to reality. Rieff notes that, despite the encouraging analogy between modern civilization and individual maturity, the future always remains pregnant with the past. If original traumas occurred in group history as well as the prehistory of the individual, then "evolution can supply no safe distance from them."[17] The recapitulation of the individual and species of the prototypal past offers testimony to the "power of the primitive in history and of childishness in the adult."[18] Rieff continues: "The primitive and the child survive in memory, the representative of the past among the faculties. Against the over-confidence of reason, representing the future, the Lamarckian Freud asserted the ancient claim of memory to a greater power than reason had allowed."[19]

The kairotic events of our prehistory—primal crimes and their repetition—are (over)preserved through the historical tradition by the force of repression. In the case of both the individual and society, the primal deed/wish must be denied, forgotten in order to persist in the unconscious. Not only does embryonic development recapitulate racial development, but thanks to the weight of tradition, the prehistorical crimes of our ancestry are reenacted in a ritual drama that continues to the present day.

If all human history is case history—the trail of the prototype, the return of the repressed—then we find only the tyranny of the past in apparent historical change. "Thus," concludes Rieff, "change becomes permanence, history nature, development repetition."[20] By placing the case study at the center of psychoanalytic inquiry, I have tried to give the connections between Freud's narratives and historical method their due. Because each life story is unique, it must be organized around a set of symbols which are highly individual, possess a density of meaning or polysemy, and fit contextually into an overdetermined narrative. Rieff counters that the "unlimited harvest of memories, associations, and symbols are collated *thematically*, independent of their time sequence."[21] Although the symbolic quality of a patient's speech or symptoms presents the opportunity for interpretation in a local context, the ability to let one thing stand for another also enabled Freud to reduce the diversity and sweep of history to the repeated expression and renunciation of libidinal wishes.

Kenneth Burke has located this interpretive rift within Freud's own thought and concludes that psychoanalysis "fluctuates in its search for an essence."[22] His reliance on free association and linguistic context for discerning meaning indicates a "proportional" mode of interpretation at odds with the "essentializing" strategy illustrated by *Totem and Taboo*. A historical interpretation is one which acknowledges that the same symbol may vary greatly in its determination and significance, depending on the context in which it emerges. But Rieff rightly criticizes Freud's competing tendency to endow the sexual wish or libido with exclusive explanatory power. If the entire history of humankind is a parable of origins reenacted in our familial and societal lives, then the explanation of the complex in terms of the simple, varied in terms of the uniform, indeed betrays an antihistorical bias.

A Review of Freud's Theory of the Instincts

Although they propose conflicting interpretations, both Rieff and Brown tie the psychoanalytic conception of history to Freud's theory of instinctual life. Brown identifies repression of instinctual wishes as the source of historical consciousness, whereas Rieff argues that history as a realm of temporal change and diversity is only manifest content which reduces and translates into the latent content of timeless and indestructible drives. For Brown, therapeutic cure consists in the abolition of history; for Rieff, the intransigence of instinctual conflict—its timeless, permanent character—is precisely what condemns humankind to neurosis as the condition of being human.

Brown, I think, is correct in maintaining that instinctual ambivalence is a human prerogative, and Rieff makes a strong case that Freud strains the sense of history when he assimilates the study of our collective past to mass psychology. However, these claims rest upon a certain understanding of what Freud meant by instinct, a notoriously slippery, ambiguous concept. The status of history in psychoanalysis cannot be ascertained until we have examined more closely the nature and function of instinctual conflict.

The definition of instinct as a psychoanalytic term varies according to the German word from which it is translated. *Instinkt* connotes hereditary behavior patterns or attributes which humans share with lower forms of animal life.[23] The term implies to the biologist phylogenetically predetermined and automatic patterns of arousal, adaptation, and action that are uninfluenced by learning. The other sense of instinct derives from *Trieb*, which translates as drive and consists in a dynamic pressure that directs the organism toward an end.[24] Instinct defined as drive is clearly the preferred meaning in Freud's writings, although the overt biologism of "Beyond the Pleasure Principle" tends to obscure the distinction between *Instinkt* and *Trieb*. Even when *Trieb* is clearly distinguished from *Instinkt,* questions about the status of the former remain. Is it essentially a biological or somatic force, a symbolic or representational activity, or the principle of interaction between mind and body? "Instinct," Freud surmised, "is on the frontier between the mental and somatic, representations of stimuli originating from within the organism and reaching the mind, as a measure of the demand made upon the mind for work in consequence of connection with the body."[25] Instinct (*Trieb*) intersects the opposition of body and mind, force and meaning, as the primary concept that grounds both the energetics model and the hermeneutical practice of psychoanalysis as a semantics of desire.

Meaning and force coincided for Freud in a psychical representative (*Repräsentant*) that stands for the instincts, but representation should not be construed as a conscious idea (*Vorstellung*). The unconscious is itself the source of all translations of instinctual life which surface in consciousness. Precisely because the representatives of the instincts are themselves forced back into the unconscious, we have no direct way of knowing the nature of instinctual life. Hence, Freud must conclude that "The theory of the instincts is so to say our mythology."[26] Instinct, in other words, is known only by its manner of functioning—its aims and objects—in the economy of mental life. Even if we designate instinct as energy, drive, or tension, "we cannot say that instincts are expressed by ideas," insists Ricoeur, "[for] this is only one of the derived aspects of representative functions of instincts. More radically it must be said that instincts themselves represent or express the body to the mind."[27] By laying bare the work of repression, according to Ricoeur, psychoanalysis reveals the "energetic vicissitudes of the instincts com-[ing] to language as the vicissitudes of their psychical expressions."[28] The instincts were inferred by Freud from their symbolic expressions in his clinical studies of mental disorders. The metapsychology, in turn, represented an effort to systematize the data gathered and interpreted in psychoanalysis. The heuristic models came to include four distinct points of view: dynamic (What is struggling for expression and what is repressing it?); genetic (How does psychical conflict develop over time?); economic (What is the distribution of libido?); and the topographical (What are the interrelationships and functions of the psyche's various components?). No single model was seen as adequate to explain the mind; nor could they be reduced to one another.[29]

The theme of instinctual conflict pervades the metapsychology. I will attempt to follow two interwoven strands of inquiry that run through the fabric of Freud's theory. The first is the development of Freud's topographical theory from the simple opposition of the unconscious to the preconscious-conscious (Uc/Pcs-C) in The Interpretation of Dreams (1900) to the tripartite model of The Ego and the Id (1923). The second is the notion of instinctual polarity, which I will trace from its early expression in hunger versus love to the "battle between the giants," Eros and Thanatos, in "Beyond the Pleasure Principle."

In the earlier topographical model, Freud located primitive instinctual wishes in the unconscious and attributed their remoteness from consciousness and the preconscious to a censor who stands along the border separating the unconscious from the preconscious region of the self. Instinctual representatives observed and interpreted in therapy—dream reports, symptoms, fantasies, parapraxes, transference—were all regarded as disguised instinctual expressions which successfully escape the censor. This was an elegant model because it paired the repressed content with the primary process under the aegis of the unconscious, while the repressing agency was identified with the secondary process presiding over the preconscious /conscious region of the self.

Despite the simplicity of the identification of the unconscious with the primary process and preconscious/conscious with the secondary process, the thesis could not adequately explain how the dynamically unconscious fantasies associated with neurotic symptoms could exhibit the logical structure characteristic of the secondary process. This imperfection in his model led Freud to admit in his 1915 paper "The Unconscious" (*Unbewusste*) that consciousness cannot serve as a criterion for the differentiation of the systems.[30]

Another shortcoming of the model arose from Freud's clinical experience of psychic resistance. Freud envisioned the censor as a barrier set up at the boundary of the preconscious to protect it against incursions from the unconscious. But his discovery of unconscious resistance in the patient's transference neurosis suggested that an individual may be no less unaware of the agent of repression than of the repressed content. Both the repressing force and the repressed must therefore be regarded as dynamically unconscious, but since Freud had located the repressing force (i.e., censorship) in the preconscious system, he now faced a direct conflict between the dynamic and systematic conceptions of the unconscious.

In *The Ego and the Id* Freud proposed a modified model of the mind whose components were not defined primarily by their relationship to consciousness. This second topographical model postulated three agencies of the self: the id (*das Es*), the ego (*das Ich*), and the superego (*das Uberich*). The ego inherits some of the functions of the preconscious and conscious systems. As the executive agency of the psyche, the ego directs and controls behavior while taking into account the dictates of both external reality and the instinctual impulses arising from within the organism. It tends to be reality oriented, like the pre-conscious, but the ego differs from the latter, since it is also responsible for dynamically unconscious activities such as fantasy formation and resistance. Much of the ego, in a word, is unconscious.

Freud found his contrast of the ego in the id, a component that produced the conflict he believed was at the core of human behavior. The id was identified with a region of mind that is both unconscious and governed by the primary process. Although the id and ego engage in conflict, they should not be regarded as sharply demarcated forces or systems within the psyche. Instead, Freud adopted a genetic point of view which conceptualized psychological development as a gradual progression toward mature differentiation and structure. From this perspective, the id exists prior to the ego. In the course of development, a certain part of the id becomes structured and forms an ego through interaction with the external world. Stated somewhat differently, the ego gradually evolves from the undifferentiated id, shades into the id when fully developed, and possesses within itself a dynamic unconscious component.

Finally, the tripartite model introduced the agency of the superego for clarification of the repressing agency as the internalized authority of parental demands and prohibitions. The superego protects the self from the ultimately self-destructive impulses of the id by exercising restraint and discipline. However, the superego tends to be punitive and gratuitous in imposing restrictions upon the id even when its wishes can be satisfied without harm to the ego. The besieged ego must constantly mediate between the infantile desires of the pleasure-seeking id, the mandates of the superego, and the demands of external reality.

[The ego] owes service to three masters and is consequently menaced by three dangers: from the external world, from the libido of the Id and from the severity of the Super-ego. . . . As a frontier-creature, the Ego tries to mediate between the world and the Id, to make the Id pliable to the world and, by means of its muscular activity, to make the world fall in with the wishes of the Id.[31]

Freud's earliest image of intrapsychic conflict was drawn, not from the energetics model, but from the mythical opposition between hunger and love. In this view, sexual or libidinal drives which promote group preservation clash internally with nonsexual, self-preservative drives. This dichotomy was soon threatened, however, by the concept of primary narcissism which undercut Freud's effort to classify the instincts according to their respective objects. The thesis that the reservoir of instinctual energy is distributed between two primary sets of drives—self-directed drives governed by the pleasure principle and socially directed drives governed by the reality principle—was contradicted by the idea of undifferentiated libido predating the distinction between self and other. If, in other words, the original libidinal cathexis is the ego and all subsequent attachments result from the progressive differentiation of self and world, then both the self and group preservative drives must derive from the *monism* of primary libidinal instincts.[32]

The concept of primary narcissism enabled Freud to reformulate the concept of instinct in terms of three drive components: source (a bodily stimulus), aim (elimination of tension obtaining at the instinctual source), and object (whatever satisfied the aim).[33] The economic point of view now defined object as a function of aim and not the other way round. As a consequence, the "object" becomes variable and contingent upon the vicissitudes of the individual's libidinal history. For example, in the pair masochism-sadism, the aim of causing pain characterizes both phenomena, but the object of masochism redirects the current of sadism against the agent's own ego. The pair can be understood without reference to choice or value but simply as the distribution and redistribution of libidinal energy.

The next significant revision of Freud's dualism appeared with the publication of "Beyond the Pleasure Principle" in 1920. Once again the image of instinctual polarity was drawn from mythology, this time in the figures of Eros and Thanatos.

In this, perhaps Freud's most audacious and speculative work, the instincts were divided according to their respective *aims:* Eros toward life as an ever-increasing unity; Thanatos toward death and reduction of tension to a zero, inorganic state. Although instinctual dualism was an a priori requirement for psychoanalysis, the argument of "Beyond the Pleasure Principle" proceeded chiefly from clinical observations which seemed to contradict the pain-pleasure and reality principles underlying the economic model. Pleasure, Freud observed in the "Scientific Project," consists in the dissipation of tension or avoidance of the painful accumulation of stimuli. The reality principle which checks psychic inertia and ensures homeostasis is, in effect, a modification of the pleasure principle, since the enforced postponement of satisfaction and even "temporary endurance of pain [are] on the long and circuitous road to pleasure."[34] The earlier theory had equated ego instincts with the reality principle and sexual instincts with the pleasure principle; the sexual instincts are normally tamed by the ego in the interest of self-preservation, but pleasure, however delayed, remained the psyche's ultimate aim. This theory, Freud discovered, fails to account for numerous instances in which pain alone and not pleasure appears to be the underlying purpose of certain kinds of behavior. The repetition of painful repressed scenes in the therapy hour, catastrophic dreams in patients suffering traumatic neurosis, and the staged experience of loss in children's games—none of these phenomena conformed with Freud's thesis that the psyche seeks pleasure through the reduction of tension.

These clinical phenomena not only challenged the primacy of the pleasure principle, they also suggested to Freud a fundamental desire for self-mastery, manifested as the effort to seize control over a situation initially experienced from a passive or powerless position. Because the child is distressed that his mother periodically leaves the house without him, he stages his mother's disappearance (throwing the toy from the crib) and return (retrieval of the toy). The invention of the game represents the child's achievement of self-mastery: by repeating the unpleasurable experience as a game, he takes an active part in his mother's departure and thereby finds compensation for instinctual renunciation.

Self-mastery also seemed to be the motive behind the dreams of traumatic neurotics. To use the language of the energetics model, a trauma breaches the shield that protects the psychic apparatus from the flood of external stimuli. When physical pain attends the breach of the protective shield, energy is summoned from all sides to cathect the environs of the breach. An anticathexis, or withdrawal of energy, to "bind" the wound before it can do significant damage is signaled by the psyche's experience of anxiety. But if, as in the case of war neurotics, a sudden physical trauma surprises the ego so that it has no opportunity to register anxiety, repetition of traumatic scenes in later dreams would serve the purpose of mastering stimuli retrospectively, that is, by developing the anxiety whose omission originally caused the neurosis.

Although Freud did not reject self-mastery as a motive for repetition, he refined his hypothesis to fit with the energetics model. Impulses arising within the psyche were characterized as freely mobile energy pressing for full and immediate discharge. In contrast to the operation of the primary process, the secondary process has as its purpose the binding or quiescence of energy. Repetition, Freud proposed, works as a process of binding energy—maintaining equilibrium—which permits the emergence of mastery and postponement of instinctual gratification. If freely mobile energy is identified with the instincts, then how can repetition, understood as the binding or retarding of mobile energy, qualify as an instinctual phenomenon?

Freud asserted that the task of binding excitation takes precedence over the pleasure principle "not indeed, in opposition to the pleasure principle, but independently of it and to some extent in disregard of it."[35] However, his only argument consisted in an appeal to the definition of instinct as "an urge to restore an earlier state of things."[36] The conservative, regressive nature of the instincts impels humans toward earlier stages of existence. The self-preservation instinct functions to assure that the organism wills its own path to death, to an immanent end which is convertible with its preorganic beginnings. The goal of all striving or desire is "an old state of things," an initial state from which the living entity has departed and to which it strives to return by the circuitous route of growth and development.[37] The aim of life, Freud concluded, is death.

Eros and Thanatos: An "Unconscious" Philosophy of History

"Beyond the Pleasure Principle" seems a poor textual candidate for a psychoanalytic philosophy of history. The essay's only direct reference to "history" occurs in a section that cites evidence for the compulsion to repeat in the "historical determination" of spawning habits in certain fish and the migratory patterns of birds. What I have in mind by the idea of history cannot be equated with an evolutionary scheme of development that has manifestly little, if anything, to do with how humankind appropriates its past or comprehends its life as an unfolding story. Reasoning from biological principles of behavior in birds and fish to comparable patterns in humans obviously contradicts my thesis that history is a phenomenon peculiar to humans. The essay also implies an antihistorical bias in placing the theory of the instincts in the context of the energetics model first sketched in the "Project for a Scientific Psychology." Was it not precisely the perceived inadequacy of this model that led Freud to an alternative inquiry into the symbolic and historical patterns of human action?

Apart from the problem of reconciling Freud's scientism with a tacit philosophy of history, the arguments themselves have been attacked by even Freud's most ardent followers for their logical inconsistency, dearth of evidence, and fanciful flights of imagination. William McDougall, who was generally sympathetic to psychoanalytic theory, dubbed the death instinct "the most bizarre monster of all his gallery of monsters."[38] Ernest Jones spoke for the natural scientists of Freud's day when he flatly asserted that the death instinct "contradicts all biological principles," and Ernest Becker speaks succinctly for the contemporary critics of the later theory when he declares that

"Freud's tortuous formulations on the death instinct can now securely be relegated to the dust bin of history."[39]

Freud himself cautioned the reader that his hypotheses were tentative and lacked adequate empirical support. He concluded the essay by admitting that he may have overestimated the significance of repetition upon which the theory rested. "In any case," he continued, "it is impossible to pursue an idea of this kind except by repeatedly combining factual material with what is purely speculative and thus diverging widely from the empirical material. . . . One may have a lucky hit or may have gone shamefully astray."[40]

This assessment of the essay is also an apt description of the analysand's report. Following the fundamental rule of free association, the analysand blends fact and fiction, submitting to an idea and following wherever it may lead. I wish to make a wager with his detractors that Freud hit upon insights which, like patients' stories, prove upon analysis to be neither fortuitous nor without underlying significance. Following a line of reasoning drawn by Peter Brooks, I propose that the instinctual character of repetition organizes for Freud the human experience of time and significance as the vacillation between beginnings and endings.[41] The concept of repetition which pushed Freud "beyond" the pleasure principle forms a natural bridge between the case studies and metapsychology.

Freud speculated that all instincts share the fundamental property of repetition compulsion (*Wiederholungzwang*) which goes beyond—is more primitive than—the pleasure principle. Within his modified theory of the instincts, the death instinct (Thanatos), manifested in the compulsion to repeat painful experiences, conflicts with the libidinal drives as representatives of the life instinct. But if the ultimate aim of the death instinct is regression to a state of complete quiescence, the absolute reduction of tension, what becomes of the libidinal drives which were previously defined by the identical function of tension reduction? The sexual instinct must be independent of the compulsion to repeat identified with the operation of the death instinct. Otherwise, Freud's instinctual dualism would once again threaten to collapse into an unacceptable monism. Yet to qualify as an instinct, it, too, must exhibit a conservative tendency.

It was only after a lengthy discussion of biological research into sexual reproduction in primitive organisms that Freud resorted to mythopoesis for insight into the origins of sexuality. According to Aristophanes' myth in Plato's *Symposium*, the sexual unity of primordial man (Androgyne) was fractured by Zeus. The coupling of male an female, Freud speculated, strives to recover this mythical unity. Eros of the poets and philosophers binds all living things, draws them together in an evolving organic whole. Freud assigned to the libidinal drives (Eros) the task of binding instinctual impulses which impinge upon the psyche, converting freely mobile energy into a quiescent cathexis. Binding, he concluded, is not opposed to the death instinct but made subservient to it. Eros represents a kind of foreplay, a preliminary maneuver that sustains excitation as the organism presses for catharsis in the pleasure of its ultimate discharge—death.

It is appropriate, I think, that Freud finally turned to myth to preserve the essentially dramatic unity and tension of life and death. The language of cathexis and anticathexis mingles with myth and drama in a mixed discourse needed to represent the language of desire. Notice that biological and poetic modes of discourse now share a metaphorical status: neither discourse is privileged because the psyche, understood as a textual economy, cannot be identified literally with either domain to the exclusion of the other. Following Lacan, Peter Brooks combines the linguistic and energetic dimensions of the psyche in a figure of speech when he says, "Repetition works as the binding of textual energies that allows them to be mastered by putting them into serviceable form within the energetic economy of narrative."[42] Binding, he continues, supplies the necessary suspense and duration to keep the story of a life from "collapsing into the nonnarratable states of beginning and ending." The vacillation of the middle, its shuttling back and forth between provisional beginnings and endings, characterizes the process that Freud described as binding. This concept relates the phenomenon of repetition directly to the theory of the instincts elaborated in "Beyond the Pleasure Principle."

We have already seen how repetition operates in psycho-analytic narrative from both the armchair and the couch. The analysand bitterly repeats through his or her transference neurosis infantile desires that have been denied satisfaction in adult life. The analyst, in turn, seeks to substitute for the analysand's unwitting interpretation of the past a comprehensible story that retells the patient's history and culminates in the reconstruction of primal scenes at the origin of the illness. Repetition in a clinical setting has, in a word, two moments: the pathological gesture of transference (reenactment) and the curative gesture of narrative diagesis (recollection of a journey already made).

The distinction between therapeutic and pathological modes of repetition becomes blurred, however, when we recall the compulsive quality of Freud's search for a satisfactory ending to the story of the Wolf Man. His desire for mastery of the patient's history was frustrated by the indeterminacy of prehistorical origins. The compulsion to repeat, which prompted Freud's formulation of the death instinct, was never entertained as a phenomenon present in his own narrative constructions. Yet the passion that animates us as readers and Freud as author/editor is no less a desire for the end.

The connection between desire for narrative closure and Freud's death instinct hinges upon the thesis, argued convincingly by Peter Brooks, that the narrative impulse present in art also operates in life. Beginnings, middles, and ends are not merely fictional plot episodes but configurations of desire. The desire for an ending may be described as a search for self-identity in the figure of a story. Our autobiographies, the stories we tell about ourselves, can never achieve closure except through the fictions by which we assess our lives retrospectively, that is, from the standpoint of our imagined deaths. Stories delimit life by imagining determinate beginnings and endings that can be otherwise known only as the indeterminate horizons that frame human experience.

Of course, it can be argued that art differs essentially from life in its insistence upon recasting contingencies as ordered, purposeful episodes that terminate in a resolution. Fictional plots typically move toward a predestined *telos* even though man's faith in a providential history has been lost. Twentieth-century writers such as Alain Robbe-Grillet have attempted to make literature "truer" to life by eliminating the contrivance of fictional time and punctuating their novels with the contingencies that riddle human existence. Yet the stubborn refusal to assimilate the unnarratable into story arguably betrays the natural impulse in life to see events, like the disparate clues of the detective story, as pregnant with significance. The historian, like the author, habitually recasts early events as prefiguring significant episodes that follow.

The appetite for narrative order which marks the beginning of a suspenseful story—or a distinctively human life—is precisely a desire for the end; and the process of transformation along the way is a "working through," a kind of suspense or detour between origin and end that constitutes a life span as plot in progress and regress. As Brooks reminds us, the idea that every beginning presupposes an end is captured by Sartre's remark that in writing *Les Mots,* the story of his life and vocation, "I became my own obituary."[43] The desire for meaning thus projects humans toward their end as both *telos* and extinction; for the story of a person's life can be read in its entirety only in the retrospective light of an ending that confers meaning and coherence on beginnings and the critical middle.

The identification of self with story presented to Freud the problem of biographical truth and narrative adequacy. "Biographical truth," he penned to Stefan Zweig, "is not to be had."[44] Psychoanalysis sought to understand psychical reality which, again, "in its innermost nature is as unknown as the reality of the external world."[45] The truth of a life, as Sartre's Roquentin confirmed in his disintegrating study of a minor historical figure, inevitably eludes the biographer's grasp:

> I am beginning to believe that nothing can ever be proved. These are honest hypotheses which take the facts into account: but I sense so definitely that they come from me, and that they are simply a way of unifying my own knowledge. Not a glimmer comes from Rollebon's side. Slow, lazy, sulky, the facts adapt themselves to the rigor of the order I wish to give them: but it

remains outside of them. I have the feeling that I am doing a work of pure imagination.[46]

The problem of the past's intractable "otherness" here reasserts itself—but with a difference. Roquentin's doubts about the validity of his project spring from the recognition that a fissure between living and telling riddles his own history, that his own identity is no less likely than Rollebon's to slip away beneath his gaze:

> For the most banal even to become an adventure, you must (and this is enough) begin to recount it. . . . he tries to live his life as if he were telling a story. Nothing happens when you live. There are no beginnings. . . . Neither is there an end. . . . But everything happens when you tell about life; it's a change no one notices: the proof is that people talk about true stories. As if there possibly could be true stories; things happen one way and we tell about them in the opposite sense. You seem to start at the beginning: "It was a fine autumn evening in 1922. I was a notary clerk in Marommes." And in reality you have started at the end. It was there, invisible and present, it is the one which gives to words the value and pomp of a beginning. . . . I wanted the moments of my life to follow and order themselves like those of a life remembered. You might as well try to catch time by the tail.[47]

Sartre's Roquentin insists that autobiographical truth is no less problematical than the story of his, or any, historical subject. Brooks observes that the autobiographical truth, understood as the "talking cure," is an elusive, interminable task precisely because it is coterminous with life as a forward movement (metonymy) which elucidates the present by showing its roots in the past (metaphor). "Human life," he writes, "is a desire for the end, but the end reached through the plot of narrative."[48] He elaborates this dramatistic model of life as plot by transposing Freud's instincts into the linguistic operations of metonymy and metaphor, the two axes along which the elements of language may be plotted.[49] Although this distinction originates in Quintilian's rhetoric, it has been modified by Roman Jakobson and exploited by Lacan in the interpretation of Freud.[50] Stated simply, metonymy is the axis of contiguity and combination, and metaphor the axis of selection or substitution. For example, in the association of Napolean's battle with a small Belgian village, "Waterloo" is formed along the metonymical axis of combination and contiguity. This linguistic operation corresponds to what Freud termed "displacement" in his early account of symptom formation and repression. Now, if a previously unsurpassed athlete "met his Waterloo," then we would have an instance of condensation in which the signifier, already carrying metonymic associations, substitutes for the term "defeat." In metonymy, then, signifier relates to signifier along a continuous chain by proximity of association, whereas metaphor connects seemingly disparate elements because of the resemblance between them.[51]

Anika Lemaire cites a clinical example drawn from Freud's own writings which establishes a straightforward correlation between metonymy and displacement on the one hand and, on the other, between metaphor and condensation.[52] A patient suffered from pains in her lower back which she eventually associated with the word *Kreuz* (cross). Because *Kreuz* also means the sacrum or sacroiliac, Freud suspected that the symptom lodged at the bottom of the patient's back through the action of displacement. Stated differently, the relationship between the association and the symptom was one of location or metonymy. However, because her association also implied "a cross to bear," the symptom represented a substitution of physical suffering for moral suffering. This example closely follows my earlier description of weak and strong symbolization. Recall the case of the patient whose "slap in the face" resulted in facial neuralgia. Here, too, the metonymic association of contiguity operated in concert with the metaphorical substitution of physical suffering for morally or emotionally painful episodes in the patient's life. Physical symptoms serve in both instances as metaphors of repressed signifiers.

We also can see the work of metonymy and metaphor in the tangle of associations that constitute a case history. Both operations, it should be noted, concern the relationship between signifiers within a chain of signifiers and not between signifier and signified, in the sense that no extralinguistic or empirical event directly corresponds with its linguistic representation. Whether we attend to Emmy's memories of childhood seduction or to the Wolf Man's dream, the meaning of a series of associations resides not in any particular relationship between sign and corresponding event (i.e., primal scene) but in the coherence of the entire set of associations. Lacan makes this point when he says, "It is in the chain of the signifiers that meaning 'insists' but . . . none of its elements 'consists' in the signification of which it is at the moment capable. We are forced, then, to accept the notion of an incessant sliding of the signified under the signifier."[53]

The temporality of desire, according to Brooks, bears upon the action of this "incessant sliding" of the signified. The motor of narrative, the desire which moves us along the metonymic chain of signifiers, seeks completeness, or totality. In its forward movement, metonymy seeks to become metaphor by affirming resemblances and assimilating seemingly contingent incidents of this forward movement to a unified plot. However, the action of the plot, the suspense that sustains our interest as readers, is possible only because comprehension—in the sense of both "holding together" and intelligibility—is incomplete. Life is itself a textual plot generated by that forward-moving narrative impulse which seeks the nonnarratable (death) precisely because the totality of meaning can be "realized" only in and through the end.

Brooks thus identifies repetition, or binding, as the generation of significance, the retrospective grasp of the text of life as metaphor. Eros achieves new unities, new configurations of meaning, but only as provisional plots which arrest the satisfaction of Thanatos in its desire to reach the end of the metonymic chain. Eros and Thanatos, succession and configuration, metonymy and metaphor—the language of desire circulates in the play of all these oppositions and gives voice to humans as those who actively seek self-mastery and self-definition through the interpretation of their own life.

The "events" of life, in this reading, cannot be separated from their rendering as narrative. History *and* fiction, insofar as they speak truthfully about human life, do not eschew narrative but employ a literary form that heightens or magnifies the organization of human experience. Just as Eros and Thanatos are interdependent in their generation of a textual economy, the terms "interpretation" and "life" should not be sharply distinguished because living and telling—perhaps the most fundamental of Freud's many dualisms—together define humans as essentially beings who question the nature of their own being.

This reading of "Beyond the Pleasure Principle" is less a response to Rieff and Brown, an assessment of their claims, than a rethinking of the concepts guiding their analysis of Freud. Rieff and Brown both adopt the idea of history as a succession of discrete events moving from the past into the present, as well as the method of inquiry into a remote past whose effects dominate the present. Rieff images Freud's scheme of development as a circle because the action of remote events (i.e., traumas) is repeated in their effects (symptoms, transference). Brown also views history in this manner but goes on to prescribe an antidote to time that will stop desire—and repression—in its tracks.

"Beyond the Pleasure Principle" intimates an idea of history, not as an exterior event or as a disinterested method of inquiry, but as a structure of memory and anticipation which "stretches out" or historicizes life between the poles of birth and death. Repetition, in this view, does not reproduce the past or capture its photographic image. Instead, the psyche's interpretive arc projects its end and from the future bends back to recollect the plot of its life as a provisional whole.

How well does Brooks's reading accord with Freud's own remarks on the relationship between our sense of an ending and biographical truth. Freud insisted that the action of therapy actually expands the bounds of the analyzable and enriches life by deepening and broadening the dimensions of self-identity. But he also hinted that our stories and case histories are regulative fictions, since all endings mark a tentative limit that will be surpassed and because lived beginnings are not the promises and annunications of literature. Death, the one limit that cannot be surpassed, is ultimately what makes the identity of self and story impossible. The attraction of drama, Freud speculated, is that we can participate in the character's tragic demise and incorporate the experience as spectators, not as agents who suffer death ourselves:

> It is an inevitable result . . . that we should seek in the world of fiction, of great literature and theatre, compensation for the impoverishment of life. . . . In the realm of fiction we discover the plurality of lives for which we crave. We die in the person of a given hero, yet we survive him and are ready to die again with the next hero just as safely.[54]

Fiction enables me to experience the wholeness of another life as I witness its "end" while my existence is preserved intact. Death can be known only vicariously; for my death is unimaginable and whenever I make the effort, I always survive as a spectator, as if my death were the death of another.[55] Freud concluded that no one really believes in his own death or, to put the same idea differently, even the unconscious is convinced of its own immortality.[56] This statement seems to contradict the argument in "Beyond the Pleasure Principle" for the existence of the death instinct. How can humans seek to die in their own fashion—that is, how can death be understood as an *immanent* end—if neither negation nor death can be represented in the instinctual domain of the unconscious? The apparent dilemma can be resolved and Freud's intention illumined by "displacing" the problem of death from Freud's text to Heidegger's *Being and Time*.

Being-Toward-Death and the Death Instinct: History in Freud and Heidegger

The phenomenon of being-toward-death is introduced at the beginning of the second part of *Being and Time*.[57] The first part analyzes the ontological structure of *Dasein* as being-in-the-world. Dasein has the character of a being who is thrown into the world and projects his or her possibilities mainly in fascination with the items of his or her world of concern. The

Being of Dasein, as care, involves facticity, existentiality, and fallen-ness. The second part reinterprets the analysis of Dasein in the light of temporality. The manner in which Dasein comports itself toward death as the "absolute possibility of Dasein's impossibility" indicates that the Being of Dasein can be thought only within the horizon of time. In anticipatory resoluteness before its own death Dasein exists authentically as a whole, and authentic existence becomes intelligible through temporality. Ecstatic temporality—Dasein's temporalizing of time—is the meaning of Dasein's being. Understood primarily in its prospective orientation, Dasein is understood as having been thrown and coming back out of its future to assume its thrownness as its own.

Before unpacking this admittedly dense synopsis and relating it directly to Freud, it should be noted that the isolation of any one moment of Heidegger's project or section of his text risks obscuring his guiding intention, one which cannot be identified with any regional (e.g., anthropological, psychological) study of humankind. Heidegger set out to reawaken the question of the meaning of Being, a question long neglected by philosophers, who regard Being as the most general, empty, and obvious concept in their lexicon. The commonsensical nature of the question has ended philosophical questioning about the meaning of Being. Yet, as we have already seen in the thought of Freud and Nietzsche, what is "forgotten" is not necessarily abolished but operates unacknowledged—and conceivably repressed—in the self-understanding we have inherited from our tradition. For Heidegger the historicality of Dasein is inseparable from the historicality of philosophy. Since the early Greeks, he averred, the philosophical understanding of Being as presence has been axiomatic. Although the question of meaning of Being no longer perplexes philosophers, the implicit identification of Being with presence continues as Dasein's inheritance, as its self-evident mode of understanding. Dasein, like the psyche of Freud's analysis, is its inheritance, its past. Far from lying behind it, the past goes out ahead of Dasein, determining the possibilities of its Being.

The relationship between the science of ontology and Dasein's self-understanding should not be construed as the historical influence of doctrine or dogma upon everyday beliefs and attitudes. Heidegger was advancing a phenomenological inquiry, not a study in intellectual history. The central point is that Dasein is distinguished from all other beings because comprehension of its being uniquely belongs to its constitution. That humankind is a uniquely self-defining, self-interpreting animal also was the point of departure for psychoanalysis as a hermeneutics. Heidegger's analysis was arguably more radical than Freud's, however, since he was intent upon laying bare the ontological structure which defines Dasein and makes the science of ontology possible. By examining Dasein's ordinary understanding of its being as a mode of time (presence), Heidegger penetrated beneath the sediment of philosophical tradition to discover the meaning of Dasein's being in finite temporality, the horizon upon which Dasein projects the unity of past, present, and future.

The contrast between time as presence and as temporality is sharply drawn in Heidegger's existenzial analysis of being-toward-death, where he elucidated two interrelated phenomena: being-as-a-whole and being-toward-an-end. Wholeness cannot be achieved because humankind's very mode of being will not permit it. If the projection of possibilities belongs necessarily to a person's being, at the moment that nothing more remains outstanding, he or she must cease to exist. Stated differently, so long as a person is, he or she never attains wholeness, and when a person does possess it, he or she ceases to be being-in-the-world.[58] Only if we envision Dasein as a present-to-hand (Vorhanden) entity does its wholeness seem incomprehensible. Our ordinary understanding of time as a series of nows—some lying behind, one present, the others lying ahead—offers a spatial representation of totality, completeness, and ending. However, humans cannot be understood existenzially in the mode of presence. The problem, then, is initially one of distinguishing categorial from existenzial interpretations of "ending" and "being-as-a-whole."

The "end of being qua Dasein is the beginning of the being (corpse) qua vorhanden entity."[59] As in Freud's example of the dramatic hero who dies tragically on the stage, the "end" may give us the impression that we have glimpsed death and understood it. But being "with" the dead contributes nothing to our understanding of the *ontological* sense of death as the dying person's own *possibility* of being. Heidegger was consistent with Freud in maintaining that no such deputizing is possible:

> Death is something which each Dasein has to take upon its own self. Death is, so far as it is, always intrinsically its own, a peculiar possibility of being in which the very being of one's own Dasein is at stake. . . . Ontologically, my-ownness [*Jemeingkeit*] and Existenz are constitutive of death. Dying is not an event but a phenomenon to be existenzially comprehended.[60]

That death cannot be objectified as an event or final phase of life is hardly an idea unique to Heidegger. The Hellenistic philosopher Epicurus sought to quiet the fear of death by reassuring us that when a person exists, death is absent, and that when death is, the person ceases to be. On how death eludes our perceptual grasp, Wittgenstein, Heidegger's contemporary, tersely remarked, "Our life has no limit in just the way in which our visual field has no limit."[61] If the limit of our visual field could be seen, then it would not be a boundary at all but an object of inspection framed by the still unseen limit of the field. The analogy offers a "view" of death as something that cannot be directly experienced as present-at-hand but which frames or delimits human existence. Freud and Heidegger both showed that when transferred from perception to an individual's inward desire, the idea of death as limit assumes the quality of something we necessarily live *toward*. Death not only frames all possible experience but as human beings we necessarily *press against* the end.

Just as man's wholeness cannot be conceived as a not-yet to be filled up, the end cannot be understood as either cessation or consummation. Both "wholeness" and "ending" receive their meaning from the relation that humankind's mode of being bears to death as its innermost possibility of impossibility. Death exists necessarily as possibility and never as a potentiality that will one day become actual. In Heidegger's words, "The closest closeness which one may have in Being-Towards-Death as possibility is as far as possible from anything actual."[62] In proposing that humankind *is always already its future,* Heidegger gathers the ecstases of finite temporality into the ontological structure of care. These structural moments of human temporality correspond to existentiality (future), facticity (past), and present (fallen-ness). Existentiality refers to how Dasein is always ahead of itself and projects itself into its possibilities. Facticity designates humankind's character as being "already thrown" (*geworfen*) into its possibilities. In this sense humans are always their past as well as their future. Finally, in fallen-ness humankind evades the immanence of death by absorption into the everyday world of the "they-self" (*das Man*). Like the repression of a painful memory, fallen-ness betrays the inalienable presence of what is disavowed in what Heidegger deems inauthentic existence and Freud neurotic illness. And just as Freud held out the possibility of resolutely facing what has been repressed, Heidegger maintained that in anticipatory resoluteness humankind wrenches itself away from the "they" and claims its innermost possibility by acknowledging human finitude. Anticipation, unlike inauthentic being-toward-death, does not evade the truth that death cannot be outstripped; instead, by anticipating its death, humankind comes toward what it has already been: "As authentically futural, Dasein is authentically 'having been' (*gwesen*). Anticipation of one's ownmost possibility is coming back understandingly to one's ownmost 'been.' Only insofar as it is futural can Dasein be authentically as having been. *The character of having been arises, in a certain way, from the future*" (emphasis mine).[63] Anticipating death reveals the "coming toward" a future which has existed all along. Repetition, and this is the key, does not imply the reproduction of a static past but the retrieval of possibilities out of the future. Genuine repetition (*Wiederholung*), Heidegger maintained, can occur only when the anticipation of death turns humankind back to an appropriation of possibilities limited by death but also by the finitude of a present informed by one's inheritance from the past.

Heidegger deepened his analysis of finite temporality in his discussion of historicality.[64] Finite temporality was first worked out in terms of being-toward-end, but this analysis neglected the other "end" of Dasein, namely, its birth. An analysis of history should remedy this one-sided tendency by regarding humankind as "that entity which is between birth and death."[65] Certainly a meaningful comparison of Freud with Heidegger would benefit from an explanation of how "beginnings" as well as "endings" structure historical being. The importance of the primitive as determinative of historical consciousness can scarcely be exaggerated in Freud's writings. Yet Heidegger cautioned against the understanding of existence between birth and death as a finite succession of moments. This sees humankind as present-at-hand and misses the peculiar ontological constitution that makes humans not the subject of history but intrinsically temporal beings. Human temporality, according to Heidegger, does not mean undergoing a sequence of events one after the other. Nor does it refer to a temporally persisting, underlying substance whose predicates or properties change under the pressure of time. Finally, Heidegger distinguishes temporality from the accumulation of traces from the past. Notice that each of these formulations can be made to correspond with Freud's manner of description: the chain of events that form a patient's etiology, the organism that undergoes fixed stages of libidinal development, changing symptoms with the passage of time, and the notion of "memory traces" which indelibly etch experiences from the past in the unconscious.

Heidegger's alternative understanding of temporality, one which I maintain is also implicit in Freud, is characterized as a kind of "reach" or "stretch" (*Erkstreckung*) bounded by the poles of birth and death. Humankind stretches itself along—or in Freud's words, "works through"—the extremes of birth and death and unites them through acceptance of its facticity and resolute anticipation of its death.

The Self's resoluteness against the inconstancy of distraction is in itself a *steadiness [Statisgkeit] which has been stretched along*—the steadiness with which Dasein as fate "incorporates" into its existence birth and death and their "between," and holds them as thus "incorporated," so that in constantcy Dasein is indeed in a moment of vision for what is world-historical in its current Situation. In the fateful repetition of possibilities that have been, Dasein brings itself back . . . to what already has been before it. But when its heritage is thus handed down to itself, its 'birth' is *caught up into its existence* in coming back from the [unsurpassable] possibility of death . . . , if only so that this existence may accept the thrownness of its own "there" [Da] in a way which is more free from Illusion.[66]

No sooner did he provisionally account for "connectedness" than Heidegger raised the possibility that the question presupposes a poor understanding of time as a succession of discrete experiences that must be united: "Is perhaps the whole of existence stretched along in this historicality in a way which is primordial and not lost, and which has not need of connectedness?"[67] Dasein's everyday understanding of itself is dispersed in the "they" and must come to itself, pull itself together (*Zusammenholen*). In other words, Heidegger is affirming what I have described as a narrative impulse to achieve coherence or to restore the sense of narrative unity once it has been lost because of, in Heidegger's terms, an inauthentic way of life. For Heidegger, inauthenticity is identified with such threats to a narrativized life as idle chatter, curiosity, and distraction (*Zerstreutsein*). Authenticity, in turn, is captured by such terms as coherence (*Zusammenholen*), wholeness (*Ganzein*), and selfhood (*Selbstsein*). The above quotation suggests, as David Carr has observed, that the moments of distraction in which actions assume the character of "mere sequence"—the senseless progress of one thing after another—do not typify experience but rather represent the "outer limit of experience."[68]

Several points should be stressed in returning the discussion of Heidegger to Freud's metabiography. First, Heidegger and Freud both rejected the idea of death as a distant event, as a scene that can be observed by a spectator, or as a phenomenon that can be adequately explained by recourse to biology or physiology. Death cannot be represented in the unconscious because it "exists" neither as an event nor as the cessation of experience. Yet death is constitutive of life as being-toward-death or, to use Freud's terminology, as death instinct. As determinative of existence, the death instinct and being-toward-death both bring into question the human experience of time. In Freud's theory, the interdependence of life and death instincts provided the context for the experience of repetition as a model of time in which the past, to use Heidegger's words, arises from the future. This way of binding time, as opposed to the succession of instants in a unilinear sequence, narrativizes human experience. No wonder, then, that Freud's explanations of our self-interpretations would resort to the narrative format of the case history. The idea of connectedness or plot as recovery of the past has guided my study of Freud's narratives and their temporal dynamics. Case studies are exemplary "lost and found" stories that move from the dispersal of the self to recollection of one's possibilities and recovery of a sense of connectedness. Freud's thinking proceeded from the observation that the psyche is a soul divided, vacillating throughout life between the poles of acknowledgment and avoidance. Both these dispositions betray the existential constitution of time experienced as "making present" inseparable from *awaiting* and *retaining*.

The idea of repetition, I have proposed, mediated between Freud's metabiography and his case studies by accounting for the temporal structure in which human experience is itself narrativized. Ricoeur echoes Kermode's interpretation of narrative time in art when he notes that the order of time in the plot is inverted so that we read the end in the beginning and the beginning in the end: "We learn to read time backward, as the recapitulation of the initial conditions of a course of action in its terminal consequences."[69] But I doubt that he would share Kermode's underlying assumption that narrative form is not inherent in the events depicted, that narrative "superimposes" the sense of an ending on the open-ended succession of events. This sharp contrast between the contingencies of life and the (contrived) necessities of literature is misleading because it fails to recognize narrative repetition as constitutive of human experience even prior to its retelling in written fiction and history.[70]

Ricoeur suggests that the primacy of narrative may be inferred from Heidegger's use of repetition to link historicality with time "reckoning" or "within-timeness."[71] Before we measure time, we reckon with it: we "have time to," "take time to," "waste time," and so on. "Dasein," Heidegger wrote, "historicizes from day to day."[72] We experience time within the web of significance that binds us to the natural environment and to the public world into which we are thrown. Heidegger emphasized that within-timeness is not reducible to a neutral series of abstract instants, although it is susceptible to leveling by measurements that are forgetful of their natural frame of reference. Narratives, too, take place in time—reckon with time—but, as Ricoeur notes, they may also bring us back from within-timeness to historicality, from "reckoning with" to "recollecting" it. Although Freud never attempted an ontological analysis, his reliance on narrative to capture the "material itself" and his emphasis upon repetition as an instinctual phenomenon together confirmed Heidegger's existenzial analysis of time in light of finite temporality. If the psyche, understood as a textual economy, is always already narrativized, then the case history is a form appropriate to its content.

5

Freud Analyzed: A Philosophical Appraisal

Over the last twenty-five years, professional philosophers have turned to psychoanalysis as an epistemological case study. The bulk of the literature has scrutinized the method for its logical rigor, the theory for its coherence, the hypotheses for verification and empirical yield. The philosopher of science formulates rules for adjudicating knowledge claims in the belief that a common ground—a privileged language or representation of the real—unites all rational inquirers in their search for agreement. All residual statements which resist translation into the proper set of terms are cast aside as "noncognitive" or "unscientific" ornamentation. Although Freud did not formulate the ground rules of linguistic competence, he certainly knew them and defended psychoanalysis against critics who claimed—and continue to claim—that he spoke a language foreign to, and incommensurable with, normal science. At the same time, we have seen that despite his ambition to articulate a new science of humankind, strict observance of the rules would have blocked the road to inquiry.

My interest has been less to discover whether psychoanalysis is capable of satisfying the criteria of normal science than to discern how Freud's abnormal discourse has altered our conception of what it means to know a human being. Here the emphasis shifts decidedly from application of logic in the system (scientific method) to reflection upon the logic of the system which purports to ground all rational inquiry (the epistemology that animates the method). The philosophic merit of psychoanalysis does not reside in the strength of its arguments before the court of, say, Popper and Hempel, but in Freud's challenge to their authority and judgment. Stated plainly, psychoanalysis becomes philosophical not by conforming to prevailing epistemological norms but by disputing them, thereby forcing us to think again what we mean by "science" and "philosophy."

I, too, characterize psychoanalysis as a case study, though what I have in mind bears no resemblance to the positivist's diagnosis and prescription for methodological cure. Freud's inquiry pressed against the limits of the Galilean model of science, but he ironically sensed failure—his *own* limitations—when the practice of psychoanalysis showed what it could not say successfully; namely, that the epistemology originating in the scientific revolution of the seventeenth century labored under the mistaken assumption of a univocal method and vocabulary for attaining knowledge. Freud's career displayed all the symptoms of a dis-ease, a crisis in self-understanding that continues to this day. Although the illness has not abated, it seldom intrudes upon the consciousness of social scientists so imbued with the myth of certitude that they believe the study of humankind to be in its infancy and vainly hope that a latter-day Galileo will soon deliver them from ignorance and triviality. Lewis Coser proved an exception to the rule when, in his 1975 presidential address to the American Sociological Association, he hinted that our obsession with grounds for certain knowledge has less to do with the mechanics of cure than the etiology of illness.

> Preoccupation with method has led to neglect of significance and substance. And yet, our discipline will be judged in the last analysis on the basis of the substantive enlightenment which it is able to supply. . . . If we neglect that major task, if we refuse the challenge to answer these questions, we shall forfeit our birthright and degenerate into congeries of rival sects and specialized researchers who will learn more and more about less and less.[1]

Rather than offering a set of solutions to the standard epistemological problems, Freud, I believe, has enabled us to place the classic picture within a larger frame. We can now see that he struggled against the belief that a single paradigm—Galilean or otherwise—could prescribe the conditions and procedures for rational inquiry into the nature of humankind. To do so, as Coser suggests, risks oversimplifying the issues and narrowing the range of inquiry to what is humanly insignificant.

In the following pages, I wish to reiterate the following claims regarding Freud's attempt to formulate a science of humankind. First, psychoanlaysis suggests an ideal of reflection that rivals the Galilean model—and cannot be reconciled with it. As a form of *poesis* (narrative construction) and *praxis* (the labor of reflection in analysis), psychoanalysis upsets time-honored, seemingly ironclad distinctions between fact and value, theory and practice, explanation and interpretation. Further, psychoanalytic interpretations are never simply right (demonstrated) or wrong (false), only more or less compelling than alternative readings which seek to redescribe an action, emotion, or situation. Finally, I characterize psychoanalysis as a moral science in which self-knowledge is achieved through personal effort—struggle against ignorance and commitment to truth—for the purpose of "reemplotting" one's life. Through conversation the inquirers seek edification without recourse to neutral explanatory procedures. We may ask whether all rational inquiry proceeds in a similar fashion.

Because he never broke the spell of classical epistemology, Freud remains a case history for philosophy rather than a pivotal figure in its tradition. Had he appreciated the significance of his "failure"—had he made his unconscious fully conscious— Freud might have joined the ranks of Nietzsche, Wittgenstein, and Heidegger, who offered corrective therapy to those systematic philosophers bewitched by the fiction of a privileged representation of the real, whether this takes the form of a Platonic *Eidos*, being as presence, logical maps of depiction, prehistoric origins, or a univocal scientific method. All human knowledge is conditional, and the conditions of experience are subject to change. A philosopher sensitive to history and to the mutations in language can appreciate the inadequacy, or partiality, of any picture of the world that claims completeness and veracity. Freud desired a foundation for his science, but like his contemporaries Heidegger and Wittgenstein, he felt the ground shifting beneath his feet.

Science and Its Discontents

In the preceding chapters, I have emphasized three interrelated issues regarding the epistemological status of Freud's aspiring science: the methodological unity of the sciences, the appropriate logic or *form* of scientific explanation, and the testability of particular propositions or hypotheses. Hempel's covering law model, I have argued, is ultimately unsuccessful in its attempt to articulate a set of formal requirements which would apply indifferently to any account that claims explanatory power. Psychoanalysis, once again, intimates an alternative form of explanation, one which is more akin to narrative (re)construction than the deduction and prediction of events from specifiable initial conditions and universal laws.

Does psychoanalysis therefore fall outside the bounds of scientific enterprise? Much depends on how we sort out two key terms: "rationality" and "science." If we discredit psychoanalysis as a pseudoscience because it cannot satisfy Hempel's explanatory requirements, then methodological unity may be enforced by refusing alternative accounts which challenge the prevailing norms of the scientific community. Or we may simply concede that psychoanalysis and such fields as history and anthropology are rational but unscientific species of explanation which more properly belong to the humanities. Yet a third possibility is that psychoanalysis is indeed a science but one which bears little resemblance to an exemplar such as physics.

Even if we concede that psychoanalysis may be scientific without exhibiting the logical form of explanation found in other sciences, we still must address the third issue mentioned above. It would be reasonable to stipulate that Freud's case histories—let alone a general theory of the mind—merit serious consideration only if their interpretations of mental life could be tested for truthfulness and accuracy. Verification is a fair expectation but one which is generally disappointed by the reader who encounters inconclusive endings to Freud's case histories. Marshall Edelson has maintained that at least some of Freud's propositions were shown to be falsifiable, citing as a prime example his discovery that the seduction scenario did not capture the biographical truth about the early life of his patients.[2] Ironically, this is perhaps the best illustration of why psychoanalytic interpretation *cannot* verify its claims. Recall the case of the Wolf Man, in which Freud advanced the seduction scenario after earlier disavowing it and then ended his narrative on a note of uncertainty regarding the status of the primal scene. Not only was he unable to determine whether the primal scene was an event or a fantasy but he was uncertain whether it finally made any difference.

Grünbaum insists that the scientific credibility of a hypothesis can be ensured only if it meets two stringent conditions. First, all findings must be deducible and predictable consequences of the hypothesis, and second, the hypothesis can be confirmed only once when alternative accounts have been discarded after extensive testing. Grünbaum argues that psychoanalysis is incapable of successfully pursuing an experimental design and charges, along with Spence and others, that its data are corrupted by suggestion and selection on the part of the analyst, by the biases of theoretical preconceptions, and by the fallibility of memory. In effect, Grünbaum argues that in order to comply with the requirement of verification, we also must invoke a univocal method of scientific inquiry. Although I acknowledge that Freud's "tally argument"—the proposal that true interpretations will be borne out by therapeutic gains— cannot substitute for veridical insight, I want to defend the position that, without Freud's conjectural method of conversation and associative connection, we would be denied access to the very material that defines the subject matter of psychoanalysis.

The last point can be brought into sharp relief by taking a closer look at how the line is typically drawn between science proper and aesthetic or practical matters which necessitate personal belief and discernment. If psychoanalysis were to pursue experimental evidence as recommended by Grünbaum, its methods of data gathering would have to be publicly observable and free of bias or distortion. Although concepts such as repression organize Freud's "data," they would possess explanatory value only if they permitted the controlled observation of variables by means of some form of measurement. Notice that this prescription for purely explicit knowledge is best carried out by the operations of a primitive computer that receives data (input), manipulates it according to the operational rules of a formal system (program), and generates the computed data (output) as no less an "external" entity than the elements that went into it.

Even if we provisionally grant that an inference machine operating on this model can generate knowledge, univocal data and procedures for manipulating the data are conditions that a wide range of rational judgments obviously cannot meet. The arts of performance, composition, and criticism are often distinguished from sciences as activities whose success cannot be ensured—and may be denied—by the application of a method or an a priori set of rules. We are familiar with the experience of a self-conscious player or artist whose performance is ruined when the rules become a theme of attention rather than the tacit component of his or her achievement. The success of our criteria, in other words, is contingent upon their use, their application in situations that require personal interpretation or discernment.

This tacit awareness is also present in our more reflective or deliberate judgments.[3] In observing a painting, we do not passively receive a datum but actively organize what we see through the spectacles of our criteria. One observer may attend to a painting's mimetic or symbolic quality, another to its composition, and both may be able to articulate their respective visions of the same painting. Now, if disagreement or misunderstanding arises between the two observers concerning the basis for aesthetic judgment, no definitive criteria—no correspondence rules—can be summoned to settle the dispute which are not themselves open to interpretive debate. Even if two critics reached a consensus on the key terms relevant to aesthetic judgment, their respective application of criteria to the same works of art would at least sometimes differ sharply. As Charles Taylor observes, on such occasions an appeal is made not to other criteria but to the context—the field of meaning—of the singular painting in which each tries to bring the other to his or her own way of seeing things.[4]

Psychology similarly attempts to illuminate the underlying sense of meaningful human expressions within the field of language. The sense of an action, Taylor continues, resides specifically in the "coherence between the actions of the agent and the meaning of the situation for him."[5] Aided by context we try to understand the agent's intentions in discerning what he or she is feeling or doing. Because an action is characterized partly by the way the agent sees the situation, by the purpose envisaged, personal interpretation—and judgment—appears to be essential to both the constitution of (speaking) subjects and rational inquiry into human behavior. Oliver Sacks, a psychiatrist who skillfully combines neurology and clinical observation, admonishes modern psychology for eschewing the practice and study of judgment:

> Neurology and psychology, curiously, though they talk of everything else, almost never talk of "judgment"—and yet it is precisely the downfall of judgment which constitutes the essence of so many neuropsychological disorders. Judgment and identity may be casualties—but neuro-psychology never speaks of them. . . . And yet . . . judgment is the most important faculty we have. Judgment must be the *first* faculty of higher life or mind—yet it is ignored or misinterpreted by classical (computational) neurology. Of course, the brain *is* a machine and a computer—everything in classical neurology is correct. But our mental processes, which constitute our being and life, are not just abstract and mechanical, but personal as well—and, as such, involve not just classifying and categorizing, but continual judging and feeling also. If this is missing, we become computer-like, as Dr. P [a patient who could not form judgments regarding the concrete, the personal, and the real] was. . . . Our cognitive sciences are themselves suffering from an agnosia essentially

similar to Dr. P.'s. Dr. P. may therefore serve as a warning and a parable—of what happens to a science which eschews the judgmental, the particular, the personal, and becomes entirely abstract and computational.[6]

Perhaps the psychologist avoids the concept of judgment because it eludes so-called "normal" science. If the psychologist has no access to brute data, neither can he or she invoke univocal or mechanical methods for judging, say, whether a person has behaved "shamefully." Taylor cautions that this does not mean we do not reach widespread agreement about the accuracy of such a description, but agreement about moral behavior or works of art rests upon shared judgment.[7] If someone asks why I identify an action as shameful, I can refer to the person's avoidance of others, the aversion of his eyes, the attempt to hide the significance of his actions. In other words I move within a family of concepts and experiences which reinforce and clarify one another. However, if my interlocutor does not inhabit the same linguistic world, cannot appreciate the family resemblances, then elucidation of context will move us no closer to a shared understanding. An argument about the meaning of an action cannot be won by the manipulation of data; rather it is resolved when one person communicates insight to the other and both finally come to terms. To use the language of hermeneutics, understanding is gained not by breaking out of the circle of interpretation but by learning how to dwell within it. Taylor writes:

> But these readings [of action and situation] cannot be explained or justified except by reference to other such readings, and their relation to the whole. If an interlocutor does not understand this kind of reading or will not accept it as valid, there is nowhere else the argument can go. Ultimately, a good explanation is one which makes sense of behavior; but then to appreciate a good explanation, one has to agree on what makes good sense. *What makes sense is a function of one's readings; and these in turn are based on the kinds of sense one understands.* (Emphasis mine).[8]

If we take the text analogue seriously, then we must either

remove the study of behavior from the realm of science and lump it together with "aesthetic or practical matters"; or we must set limits upon the scope and application of the classical model in determining what constitutes a science of human-kind. Of course, the latter alternative is unacceptable to those suspicious of hermeneutics precisely because it contradicts the idea of a unified science and jeopardizes the testability of scien-tific statements. As Richard Rorty points out, although the fact that humans speak a language is no reason to think they escape the reach of predictively powerful laws, we can predict that noises will issue from someone's mouth without our knowing what they mean. "Thus even if we could predict the sounds made by the community of scientific inquirers in the year 4,000," he writes, "we should not yet be in a position to join their conversation."[9] Only by joining the conversation and speaking the agent's language can we adequately account for his or her actions. At the risk of belaboring the point, the lan-guage by which we describe the conditions for producing noise is not equivalent to the statements expressed by the noise. The incommensurability of one language with the other jeopardizes neither discourse. It does contest, however, the presumption of a single language which serves as a permanent, neutral framework for generating and testing all good explanatory hy-potheses.

Once we recognize the role of the knower in making intelligi-ble the known, we also appreciate how our evolving ideas of order, coherence, and evidence profoundly influence what we experience and how we understand. If our epistemological ideal is fully explicit knowledge, then we are naturally drawn to the understanding of humankind in the likeness of a comput-er. The problem with the analogy is its forgetfulness of the con-ditional character of criteria for knowing. Because we actively participate in shaping knowledge, and the basis of our thinking cannot be grounded in a single stratum of experience, the com-puter analogy seems as inappropriate for scientific inquiry as it is for the arts. Indeed, science itself becomes an aesthetic or practical matter if we grant that all explicit knowledge rests on the "know-how" of tacit awareness. In attempting to form explicit rules for our interpretations, we eventually must resort to rules which we merely use as tools: we dwell in them as a blind man dwells in his cane.[10] We can go on forever having rules for the application of rules for the application of rules. At some point, however, as Kant maintained, we must resort simply to "mother wit." To take the most obvious yet significant example, our comprehension of an utterance presupposes linguistic competence, an understanding of the language itself. Our knowledge may be rule-bound, but we never become fully cognizant of the conditions of our speech. It would be more accurate to say that we know through them in acts that order and unify experience. Because the tacit dimension of our thought is both cultural and historical, the conditions of thought also change. We cannot identify an ultimate set of categories precisely because people, understood as self-defining beings, are apt to change their mind.

The consequence of this position is that we can never achieve the certitude in our understanding of self or world that was demanded by the Galilean model. We need not lose faith in reason—we continue to uphold our ideas with universal intent—provided that we recognize the role of commitment and belief in all rational inquiry. I want to make it clear that the failure to ground knowledge philosophically in no way jeopardizes the work of sciences which rely upon precise methods to advance inquiry. What changes is the epistemology which accounts for that activity, one which recognizes its conditions, limitations, and ultimately interpretive character. In other words, I object solely to the normative *prescription* for appeal to brute data, wholly explicit procedures for manipulating the data, and prediction as the premier form of explanation.

Psychoanalysis, as we have seen, operated on two levels of discourse. Because he had one foot in the classical tradition, Freud gestured toward the redescription of behavior in terms of neurophysiological or pharmacological laws. A comprehensive explanation that fitted psychoneuroses with the laws of natural science certainly would *correlate* bits of behavior with the workings of the nervous system, but we may ask whether this is a satisfactory explanation that would make fully motivated be-

havior intelligible. This was Rorty's point when he distinguished the meaning of an utterance (or, in this case, a symptom) from our ability to predict where and when it will occur.
Psychoanalysis grew out of the recognition that no amount of
information about the nervous system could adequately account for the meaning and significance of neurotic symptoms,
parapraxes, or dreams. Similarly, we appreciate intelligence
not by viewing brain scans but by engaging people in conversation, chess, or problem-solving tasks. Freud was concerned that
such acts of discernment appeal to ordinary language, cannot
be replicated, and lack the methodical rigor found in, say, neu-
rophysiology. Yet the doubt persisted that the exact sciences
would neglect what needed explaining or simply explain it
away. Should the cook adopt the measurements of the chemist
if the recipe calls for a pinch of salt?[11] Should human affairs be
understood in terms of the magnitude of our concerns—a time
for every purpose—or the abstract measurements that level *kairos* in the interests of *chronos*? It all depends on the language
game that we choose to play.

Not surprisingly, the interpretations of symptoms and
dreams that today seem forced or contrived were intended to
"prove" some proposition in psychoanalytic theory.[12] To the
disciple's dismay, those interpretations that we admire for their
insight were inferences lacking in the formalized steps that can
be rehearsed at will. Even when Freud put aside his energy-
distribution model, opposing modes of *clinical* explanation
vied for his sympathy. On the one hand, he was drawn to the
Galilean model of an empirical science which could verify hypotheses by appealing to the data of human behavior. On the
other, he continually revised his basic concepts to accord with
what he had learned in conversation aimed at heightening mu-
tual awareness. Does knowledge consist in correspondence
between hypothesis and a reality apart from (yet a part of)
ourselves or in the insight that issues from psychoanalytic
dialogue?

This question has a direct bearing on the status of Freud's
metapsychology, a framework which contained assumptions
concerning the structure and function of the psychic apparatus

as well as mechanisms of the genesis of neurotic symptoms. The framework evolved from experiences in the analytic situation and was thus embedded in the context of self-reflection. From this perspective, the metapsychology was, to use a term coined by Jürgen Habermas, a "metahermeneutics" which unfolded the logic of the analytic dialogue.[13]

Once the metapsychology was detached from the analytic experience that gave rise to it, the strict requirements of the Galilean model crept into Freud's understanding of psychoanalytic theory. Although hypotheses concerning the canalizing of "mental energy" (e.g., cathexis, decathexis) could not be directly tested, Freud insisted that clinical findings could substitute for experimental verification of his instinctual economics. Kepler's astronomy, he argued, was a comparable theory in which both the laws and its consequences refer to *specific* events and objects. Consequently, both psychoanalysis and astronomy make scientific gains without the benefit of strict experiment to test their respective hypotheses.[14] The comparison is misleading, however, since the controlled observation of predicted events in astronomy cannot substitute for intersubjective inquiry into perplexing memory symbols. Stars, however luminous, are inert and silent; and observation, however powerful the lens one looks through, misses the significance of utterances spoken in conversation. Recall that Breuer withdrew from the practice of the "talking cure" because it violated the rule of neutrality and made "value-free" observation impossible. Freud soon learned that the emotional entanglements of transference—the loss of control—were essential to gaining an understanding of the analysand's symptoms and motives. The analyst is implicated in the patient's illness to the extent that he or she participates in a performance of the childhood trauma.

Ricoeur has shown how the competing epistemological aims of observation ("looking at") and conversation ("participating in") can be located with the double movement of the subject from the dispossession of consciousness through the recapture or appropriation of displaced meaning expressed in desire. Dreams, fantasies, and symptoms were all evidence of the pretension of consciousness in setting itself up as the origin of meaning. The struggle against narcissism or the false cogito led to the discovery that language must be rooted in instinctual drives. Psychoanalysis dwells on archaic patterns of desire, the persistent attachment to lost objects. The infantile wishes that have not been renounced must now be recognized, mourned, and surpassed. If the soul must be lost in order to be saved, then it is always in and through interpretation that the soul can recognize its "fallen" condition. Only by deciphering the verbal tricks of desire can the instinctual drives be discovered.

The language of force, Ricoeur insists, is necessary to account for the dynamics of conflict which ensue in dispossession of the self. Reference to causal forces, pressures, and mechanisms is commensurate with the reality of a being who is an "it" (*das Es*) developing into a "me" (*das Ich*)—a described object as well as a describing subject. However, all the pressures of desire are articulated in the vocabulary of significant dreams, symptoms, and associative memories. If instinctual economics is necessitated by the phenomenon of dispossession, evidence of repression surfaces only when the illusions have been recognized so that the subject may be found. Symptoms and verbal slips betray the force of repression but always in terms of their significance for an agent. To take a recent example from my own experience, the representative of a hospital thanked a donor for his generosity and informed him that the hospital would commemorate a "plague"—as opposed to "plaque"—in his honor. Unless we dismiss such slips as meaningless word-processing errors, it is difficult to comprehend the hospital representative's behavior except in terms of emotional ambivalence and the agency of repression. Nor is it apparent how such conflicting impulses can be disclosed—especially when the agent's distorted wish eludes consciousness—except within a field of symbolic action where rival interpretations contend for our assent. Far from conducting impartial tests of alternative hypotheses, psychoanalysis requires that we assess the plausibility of conflicting interpretations through the exercise of discernment or judgment on the part of the analyst, analysand, or the reader—in short, of anyone who joins the conversation.

This explains the frustration on the part of those who are wedded to the Galilean model.

From Science to Philosophy

Late in his career, Freud remarked that the legacy bequeathed by psychoanalysis would prove to be the clinical method, important less for its application to neurotic patients than "on account of the truths it contains, on account of the information it gives about what concerns human beings most of all—their nature—and on account of the connection it discloses between the most different of their activities."[15] How is this information imparted and to whom? What is the "nature" of which Freud speaks? Finally, what connections are disclosed by psychoanalysis? We can attempt to answer these questions either by explicating the hypotheses and doctrines contained in Freud's writings or by returning to the analytic situation as an adventure of reflection which moves beyond the treatment of repressed Viennese women.

> Psychoanalysis sets out to explain . . . uncanny disorders; it engages in laborious investigations . . . until at length it can speak thus to the ego:
> A part of the activity of your own mind has been withdrawn from your knowledge from the command of your will. . . . you are using one part of your force to fight the other part. . . . A great deal more can be known to your consciousness. *Come, let yourself be taught!* . . . *You may cherish the illusion that you learn of all the more important things.* But in some cases, as that of instinctual conflict . . . your intelligence service breaks down. . . . In every case, the news that reaches your consciousness is incomplete and often not to be relied on. You behave like an absolute ruler who is content with information supplied by the highest official and never goes among the people to hear their voice. *Turn your eye inward, look into your depths, learn to know yourself.* [Emphasis mine.][16]

If the Socratic admonition cannot be followed outside the an-

alytic situation, we may ask whether psychoanalytic and Socratic dialogue share a common aim. As Shoshona Felman observes, both Freud and Socrates engaged in dialogue with
students; both also declared their ignorance and the impossibility of teaching.[17] Is the disavowal of authority the radical
condition of education as one of the "impossible professions"?
Freud expressed this paradoxical conviction when he wrote, "It
almost looks as if analysis were the third of the 'impossible'
professions in which we can be sure beforehand of achieving
unsatisfying results. The other two which have been known
much longer are education and government."[18] Freud was oc-
cupied with the business of healing, but the three professions
are of the same depth, mutually implying and reinforcing one
another. To govern means to exercise self-control, and when the
soul is afflicted with ignorance and disorder, it must be healed
to be made whole. Education, I think, can be characterized as
an activity of reflection which joins learning to a condition of
the soul.

The suggestion of a kinship between psychoanalysis and Platonic dialogue goes against the grain for several reasons. If Plato's interlocutors searched after the nature of excellence (arete),
Freud's case studies exposed the pretension of consciousness to
knowledge and virtue; if Plato recognized the telos of reason to
be the Good, Freud shattered the idols of religion and metaphysics as infantile attachments to be surpassed in maturity. In
short, if Plato represented the triumph of rationality, Freud reminded us of its limits and its subservience to the tricks of desire. From certain statements made by Freud, we might even say
that the purpose of psychoanalysis is to limit or to undo the
pernicious effects of education. "Accordingly, education must
inhibit, forbid, suppress [the instincts] and this is abundantly
seen in all periods of history. But we have learned from analysis
that this suppression of instinct involves the risk of neurotic
illness."[19] Against this conventional, one-sided reading of
Freud and Plato, a reading based upon explicit statements
made about education, I wish to examine the logic of inquiry
that emerges from the action of dialogue to bring psychoanalysis within the horizon of philosophic reflection. The sci-

ence of humankind, I submit, must become philosophical to achieve the kind of self-knowledge recommended by Socrates. Psychoanalysis, from the perspective of the case study, moves resolutely in this direction.

Plato's *Meno* develops both substantively and dramatically several issues important to Freud: the use of method to acquire knowledge, the requirements for definition of basic terms, and the identification of learning with recollection. These issues crystallize around the question of teaching and learning, that is, the nature of inquiry as education. The dialogue opens with Meno's question concerning the manner in which virtue is acquired. "Can you tell me, Socrates, if virtue can be taught? Or is it not teachable but the result of practice, or is it neither of these, but men possess it by nature?"[20] Socrates does not answer but raises a logically prior question, namely, What is virtue? As the dialogue progresses, Socrates brings the reader to appreciate that no strightforward definition can be provided because the logic of a concept such as excellence admits of no formula that can be committed to memory. Meno, whose name suggests "remembering" (*mnemon*), recalls the doctrines of his teacher, notably Gorgias, and relies on the faculty of memory to enumerate the multiplicity of virtues that would satisfy Socrates' request for a definition. Meno's list follows Gorgias's formula: virtue differs according to the particular functions and time of one's life.[21] A virtuous man, recites Meno, governs the city, protects his friends, and vanquishes his enemy; a virtuous woman orders the household and obeys her husband's wishes. Socrates complains that Meno's definition is like a swarm of bees: we are familiar with the workers, drones, and queen but not the essence which defines their shared nature. If bees are alike in virtue of a common end or purpose rather than some shared property, then we may inquire into how the parts contribute to the good of the whole—in this case the hive or colony.[22] Questions about virtue, about just or temperate action, similarly shift our attention from individual tasks to shared responsibilities. Meno does not catch the hint, however, and refuses to take responsibility for his words or to contribute to the dialogue in which he takes part. Instead, having discovered the inadequacy of his initial approach, he takes refuge in scientific definition, the language of the expert.

Read as a dramatic narrative, the dialogue shows more than it can say about the theme of virtue. The character of Meno represents through his actions the method of eristic reasoning: he is antagonistic, skeptical, and refuses to accept undefined terms. Socrates, by contrast, embodies the dialectical method: he is friendly ("erotic"), clarifies terms only when the conversation reaches an impasse, and genuinely seeks truth as a partner in philosophic inquiry. The dialogue exhibits the connection between knowledge and character, showing how definition is ultimately inseparable from self-definition—the shape or *eidos* of the soul. The task of educating Meno therefore involves the other two "impossible professions" as well. As "teacher," Socrates is faced with the task of changing Meno's nature so that he may govern his soul and cure his ignorance. Teaching, we shall see, is not pouring the contents of one mind into the empty vessel of another; but not until Meno's attitude changes will he be capable of learning from within.

Freud, too, was vexed by the problem of definition, especially in his investigations of psychical reality and the unconscious, and like the concept of excellence, these notions tie definition to self-definition. The language of location, place, and anatomy failed Freud in his attempt to circumscribe a reality that seemed to lack determinate boundaries and eluded the designation of "inside" or "outside." Indeed, by referring to the unconscious as a region of the mind that lurks *behind* conscious phenomena, we would hypostatize it and make it an unintelligible positivity—a second awareness that is not aware, an attic of ready-made ideas and memories awaiting retrieval. In giving up anatomy (conceptual or physical), Freud was seeking a mode of comprehension commensurate with the reality that emerged in the analytic situation. Freud's case studies make the unconscious intelligible not by explicating the concept in terms of a scientific definition but by implicating the analysand and analyst in the web of meaning spun in conversation. By articulating the grammar of belief, psychoanalysis enables the analysand to reemplot his life and thereby define himself. A parallel turn occurs in the *Meno*.

When a frustrated Meno asks Socrates to provide a definition of virtue common to freemen and slaves, he offers instead a definition of figure (*schema*) which applies equally to the contraries of roundness and straightness. Figure, quite simply, is what goes along with color. The definition is eminently clear, linking the concept to the world of common sense and saying something that strikes us as true upon reflection. The linking definition which associates one term with others in its family unifies and widens the context of understanding rather than pushing us outside the language we ordinarily speak. However, Meno objects that such a definition relies upon an undefined term—color—and so rejects it. Socrates next offers for Meno's consideration a geometric definition which makes no reference to color: figure is the limit or boundary of a solid. This definition gains clarity at the expense of abstraction, removing the concept of "figure" from the world of common experience and language. Meno is satisfied with this definition, but because his own thoughts are unconnected, he abruptly demands from Socrates an adequate definition of color, too. In keeping with the manner of Empedocles and Gorgias, color is defined as "an effluence of figure, commensurable with sight and therefore perceptible."[23] The definition is very technical, obscure, and absurdly broad. Moreover, it leaves "figure"—let alone "sight" and "effluence"—undefined, thus failing to remedy the apparent problem detected in the first definition. But Meno admires its "stately style" and prefers it to a linking definition within ordinary language. We can only speculate whether he would also appreciate Freud's more tortuous formulations in the metapsychology. What we do know is that Meno and Socrates represent competing impulses within Freud's own ambivalent mind.

After yet a third attempt at defining virtue ends in failure, an exasperated Meno declares that the "What is virtue?" question is pointless. One cannot inquire into what he knows because he already knows it; but neither can he inquire into what he does not know because he does not know where to look. This paradox rests upon a flawed understanding of education, one which is compatible with Meno's moral outlook. He confuses goodness with goods such as gold and silver that may be passed down from father to son as an inheritance. If Socrates has no wealth of wisdom to share, then Meno has no use for him and so resolves to bring the dialogue to an end. A teacher should possess expertise, which is the sole condition of education, and learning amounts to remembrance—the ability to repeat the teacher's words. Without expertise that can be imparted to another, education cannot take place.

Socrates cannot solve Meno's paradox because it presupposes an untenable dichotomy between explicit knowledge and utter ignorance. The transition from ignorance to knowledge thus becomes unintelligible because in either case what is known is some "thing" whose relation to the knower remains external and fortuitous. The importance of effort, the labor of reflection, is lost to Meno. Freud, who stressed "working through" a problem, knew better:

> It is a long superseded idea . . . that the patient suffers from a sort of ignorance, and that if one removes this ignorance by giving him information [about the causal connection of his illness with his life, about his experience in childhood, and so on] he is bound to recover. *The pathological factor is not his ignorance in itself, but the root of this ignorance in his inner resistances; it was they who first called this ignorance into being and they still maintain it now. The task of treatment lies in combatting these resistances.* (Emphasis mine)[24]

Teaching, like analysis, does not deal so much with adding to an individual's store of knowledge as with the willful resistance to knowledge. Ignorance, as Shoshona Felman has put it, is a kind of passion, "not a simple lack of information but the refusal to acknowledge one's one implication in the information."[25] Learning begins with the recognition of our own ignorance, the illusions maintained by repression and forgetfulness. An adequate account of both education and analytic cure must supply a notion of *anamnesis* that reveals the defects inherent in Meno's conception and practice of memory.

Socrates tries to combat Meno's resistances without losing his cooperation by recounting the doctrine of recollection, which holds that in the distant past, long before the birth of man, our souls learned all things. The myth suffers from the inability to explain how learning is possible—it only defers the problematical origins of education—but it moves the dialogue forward by offering a better account of learning and memory than that given by Meno. Education, according to the myth, does not impart new information but rids the soul of all beliefs which cloud vision and cause blindness. The myth also asserts that everything in nature exists in kinship with everything else, thus suggesting that it is possible to recollect the whole of nature starting from our own partial perspectives on the world. The emphasis on comprehension of the whole as a goal of reflection and as a process that bends the soul inward departs from Meno's understanding of memory as the retrieval of isolated formulas or scraps of information. Recall that the aim of analysis, too, is not merely to induce the analysand's memory of isolated events but to help him or her become capable of forming meaningful sequences and ordered connections. In short, the analysand seeks to constitute his or her own existence in the form of a story where memory as such is only a fragment of the story. It is the linguistic, and specifically narrative, structure of such efforts at recollection that makes a case a case history.

To demonstrate the doctrine of recollection, Socrates directs questions to a slave which eventually lead him to the solution of a geometry problem.[26] Once assured that the slave speaks Greek, that is, can converse in the language of reason (*logos*), Socrates confidently proceeds to free his student's ability to learn; whereas Meno, who still refuses to acknowledge the implications of his words, remains enslaved to the words (i.e., opinions) of others. The mathematical demonstration in which the slave doubles the side of the square shows how learning is possible without either retrieving temporarily forgotten information or memorizing a new set of rules. Recollections consist rather in *reordering* the concepts that one already knows (e.g., "double," "square"), in reminders which elucidate the language that one already speaks.

Knowing a thing, Socrates implies, requires that we understand the grammar of its concept, the family of terms in which the concept of, say, "excellence" is situated and made fully intelligible.[27] Similarly, the grammar of belief articulated in psychoanalysis takes the form of a text which forms new connections between words to display the structure and implications of our desires. Whether we are examining the connection between knowledge and virtue or between memory symbols in the analytic situation, attempts at definition are indissolubly bound to efforts at self-definition and self-control. Stated somewhat differently, the shape of a concept reveals the shape of the soul—for it is through language (*logos*) that we become fully human, and through ignorance/repression that our humanity is jeopardized. In Platonic dialogue the struggle against forgetfulness may be described as a conversion of the soul, in psychoanalytic dialogue as the reemplotment of a life.

Meno eventually redirects the conversation to the original question concerning whether virtue may be taught. That he even raises this question shows how little he has learned. Habituated to an impoverished view of education and forgetful that the nature of virtue must first be addressed, Meno is not yet disposed to self-reflection. Socrates nevertheless entertains the possibility that the virtuous men who have governed Athens instilled *arete* in their sons. Unfortunately, no such examples can be found—the offspring of Demosthenes and Pericles were unremarkable men—and the question remains unresolved. Yet is it not possible to govern well without the benefit of knowledge if one possesses the right opinion? Does it matter whether I know the road to Larissa if a person with the right opinion points in the same direction? Socrates now sounds the theme that returns our discussion to Freud. Right opinion, he says, is like the statues of Daedalus, which run away unless they are tied down. We can "bind" right opinion by "reflection on reason." Knowledge differs from true opinions in that it is bound or anchored as a result of the process in which "opinions" are "many times" and in "different ways" examined. This binding of true opinions is done by giving an account of them—by articulating what is otherwise known only tacitly—and this is recollection.[28]

For Freud, too, the drive toward intelligibility—the unified comprehension of the whole—was described as a form of binding which works toward the generation of significance and allows us to grasp the text of life as metonymy become metaphor. Eros, personified by Socrates in the dialogue, is characterized by Freud as the instinct tending toward combination—ordered connections—in new unities. The psyche, we said, projects toward its end—its *telos*—in order to recollect the plot of its life as a provisional whole.

We might say that the *Meno* is a failed dialogue: we never are told what virtue is, whether it can be taught, or by whom. Socrates still professes ignorance, and Meno becomes perplexed. Yet we also know that this is as it should be, because the terms of the question prohibit an answer and because Meno's perplexity indicates that he has finally refuted his previous opinions and confronted his moral and intellectual ignorance. The reader is to Plato as Meno is to Socrates. As readers, we have no answers but we are changed by the action of the narrative. We, too, should be perplexed if the purpose of instruction is ultimately to serve as a stimulus to inquiry and self-reflection. Consent to incompleteness, the absence of total and explicit knowledge, emerges as the dialogue's chief virtue.

Psychoanalysis also teaches us that learning is interminable. As Shoshona Felman reminds us, what counts in the encounter between analyst ("teacher") and analysand ("student") "is precisely the transition, the struggle-filled *passage* from one position to the other. But this passage is itself interminable; it can never be crossed once and for all."[29] The assertion that therapy/learning is without term rests, I believe, upon a conception of the unconscious which denies the very possibility of totally explicit knowledge, a consciousness transparent to itself. As Lacan writes, "The discovery of the unconscious . . . is that the implications of meaning exceed the signs manipulated by the individual."[30] Whenever we speak, we mobilize the language in more ways than we know; or putting it the other way around, we always know more than we say. Absolute knowledge is unavailable to us because articulation can never exhaust the resources of the language, the excess of signs that is necessarily mobilized by speech. Human knowledge in principle cannot be totalized, since ignorance cannot be completely eradicated. We forever

confront otherness within ourselves, but the necessity of media-
tion and the permanence of "ignorance" does not have the effect
of truncating reason. Far from it. The recognition of our ignorance, or of the illusion of the *cogito*, stimulates our desire for
self-knowledge and puts us on the road of inquiry. Moreover, our
desire is always answered by the intelligibility of the psyche,
which grants interpretation of its symbolic expressions.

My purpose for bringing Freud into dialogue with Plato is to
show how a "science of humankind" may call for self-reflection
that does not match our ordinary conception of how a science
proceeds and what it can achieve. Despite his reputation as a
debunker of philosophy and religion in favor of the reality principle and science, Freud returned us to a pattern of rationality
that had first appeared in the ancients. This pattern merges language and reason in *logos*, inscribes language in the book of the
soul, and reinstates teleology as the drive of reason to attain a
unified comprehension of self. This way of speaking obviously
shares little in common with the Galilean model of science that
psychology and the social sciences emulate and seek to extend
to our understanding of humankind.

I raised the question earlier where Freud's writings stand in
relation to philosophic discourse. By reading him in light of
Plato, we see how he may participate as one voice in philosophic conversation. We know by now that what lies in our distant
past is likely to fall outside the ken of conscious understanding—often deliberately so. As well as questioning the philosophic merit of the unconscious as a basic concept, we may
wonder whether philosophy is the unconscious core of Freud's
thinking. Does this imply that psychoanalysis was not really a
science after all? This is the kind of question posed by Meno,
since, in asking it, we presume to know the logic of the concept
(i.e., science) before we are familiar with how it can be applied.
The disputatious, clever side of Freud that reminds us of Meno
appealed to the authority of biology and physics for his models
and metaphors. He insisted upon the scientific status of his hypotheses, seeking support for them—and evidence against his
detractors' claims—in clinical findings. This side of Freud is
prominent in the summaries, introductions, outlines, and
metapsychology papers. The Socratic persona appears in the

case studies and interpretation of dreams and jokes, though even here the interpretive art is occasionally forced to serve polemical purposes. Nevertheless, like Socrates who learns from a slave, Freud learns about man, not from authority, but from the marginalia of human experience: nocturnal dreams, casual jokes and parapraxes, patients who suffer from mental illness. Are the "teachings" of the Socratic Freud scientific? According to the standard account, psychoanalysis should not be so judged. But should we accept its verdict that Freud's claims on us are devoid of truth? This conclusion stems from an epistemology that prizes method because it distrusts our ability to know the truth without removing ourselves, ironically, from its comprehension. Psychoanalysis contributes to the critique of this epistemology by showing how all knowledge is necessarily personal and far exceeds the application of exact methods.

Science, as we ordinarily understand it, provides us with an array of knowledges—like the list of virtues enumerated by Meno—but the self-knowledge promised by psychoanalysis is a reflective moment in our lives that belongs to no particular science. This philosophical impulse in his writings distinguishes Freud as a thinker and will preserve his memory long after the "sciences of humankind" have forgotten him.

Notes

Introduction

1. These approaches to Freud's writings are represented, respectively, by David Bakan, *Sigmund Freud and the Jewish Mystical Tradition* (Boston: Beacon Press, 1975); Frank J. Sulloway, *Freud: Biologist of the Mind* (New York: Basic Books, 1979); Stanley Edgar Hyman, *The Tangled Bank: Darwin, Frazer, Marx, and Freud as Imaginative Writers* (New York: Atheneum, 1974); and Bruno Bettelheim, *Freud and Man's Soul* (New York: Knopf, 1983).

2. See, for example, Sidney Hook, ed., *Psychoanalysis, Scientific Method, and Philosophy: A Symposium* (London: Evergreen Books, 1960). More recently, Adolf Grünbaum has argued that, although Freud's hypotheses conform to the canons of scientific method, they are not adequately confirmed by empirical evidence. See Adolf Grünbaum, *The Foundations of Psychoanalysis: A Philosophical Critique* (Berkeley: University of California Press, 1984).

3. René Descartes, *Discourse on Method*, trans. Laurence Lafleur (New York: Bobbs-Merrill, 1977), pp. 4, 5.

4. Ibid., p. 5.

5. Sigmund Freud, *The Origins of Psychoanalysis: Letters to Wilhelm Fleiss, Drafts, and Notes (1887–1902)*, trans. Eric Mosbacher and James Strachey; ed. Marie Bonaparte, Anna Freud, and Ernst Kris (New York: Basic Books, 1954), p. 355 (hereafter cited as *Origins*).

6. Ibid., p. 129.

7. See Paul Ricoeur, *Freud and Philosophy: An Essay on Interpretation*, trans. Denis Savage (New Haven: Yale University Press, 1970), pp. 65–67.

8. Stephen Toulmin, *Human Understanding: The Collective Use*

and Evolution of Concepts (Princeton: Princeton University Press, 1972), pp. 478, 133.

9. The classic statement of the covering law model is found in Carl Hempel, "The Function of General Laws in History," *Journal of Philosophy* 39 (January 1942), pp. 35–48, reprinted in Patrick Gardiner, ed., *Theories of History* (Glencoe, Ill.: Free Press, 1959).

10. Galieleo Galilei, "Letter to the Grand Duchess Christina. 1615," in *Dialogues Concerning the Two Greater Systems of the World.* Trans. Thomas Salisbury, included in his *Mathematical Collections and Translations,* vol. I (London, 1661). Cited in Edwin Arthur Burtt, *The Metaphysical Foundations of Modern Science* (Garden City, N.Y.: Doubleday, Anchor Books, 1954), p. 75.

11. This statement from Arthur C. Danto is cited without reference by Louis O. Mink, "History and Fiction as Modes of Comprehension," *New Literary History* 1 (1970): 544.

12. See Heinz Hartman, "Psychoanalysis as a Scientific Theory," in Sidney Hook, ed., *Psychoanalysis, Scientific Method, and Philosophy: A Symposium* (London: Evergreen Books, 1960), pp. 33–37.

13. See Ernst Nagel, "Methodological Issues in Psychoanalytic Theory," in Sidney Hook, ed., *Psychoanalysis, Scientific Method, and Philosophy: A Symposium* (London: Evergreen Books, 1960), pp. 38–56.

14. Ricoeur, *Freud and Philosophy,* pp. 344–47, 374.

15. Louis Agosta persuasively argues this point in "Intersecting Languages in Psychoanalysis and Philosophy," *International Journal of Psychoanalytic Psychotherapy* 5 (1976): 507–33.

16. See Michael Sherwood, *The Logic of Explanation in Psychoanalysis* (London: Academic Press, 1969), pp. 23–26. Sherwood systematically examines psychoanalytic narratives for their explanatory power within the framework of a science of humankind.

17. Sigmund Freud, "The Aetiology of Hysteria" (1893), from the *Standard Edition of the Complete Works of Sigmund Freud,* 24 vols., trans. and ed. James Strachey, assisted by Alix Strachey and Alan Tyson (London: Hogarth Press, 1953–67), 3:192 (hereafter cited as *S.E.*)

18. Quoted without citation by Edward Rothstein, "The Scar of Freud," *New York Review of Books* 27 (October 1980): 16.

19. Ibid., p. 16.

20. Stanley Hauerwas with David Burrell, *Truthfulness and Tragedy* (South Bend, Ind.: Notre Dame University Press, 1977), p. 28. For a thorough discussion of narrative connections that emerge as the reader follows a story from beginning to end, see W. B. Gallie, *Philosophy and Historical Understanding* (London: Schocken Books, 1964), chaps. 1–3.

21. For scrutiny of the fixation upon Oedipus complexes in literary criticism, see Stanley Edgar Hyman, *The Armed Vision: A Study in the Methods of Modern Literary Criticism* (New York: Vintage Books, 1955), p. 160. A survey of literary uses of Freud can be found in Meredith Skura, *The Literary Use of the Psychoanalytic Process* (New Haven: Yale University Press, 1981).

22. Kenneth Burke, *The Rhetoric of Religion: Studies in Logology* (Berkeley: University of California Press, 1970), p. 82.

23. Peter Brown, *Augustine of Hippo: A Biography* (Berkeley: University of California Press, 1969), pp. 175–76.

24. Augustine, *The Confessions*, 10:1. Cited in and trans. Peter Brown, *Augustine of Hippo: A Biography* (Berkeley: University of California Press, 1969), p. 181.

25. Burke, *Rhetoric of Religion*, p. 17.

26. Sigmund Freud, *Gesammelte Werke*, vols. 1–17 (London: Imago Publishing, 1940–52); vol. 18 (Frankfurt am Main: S. Fischer, 1968). I also consult on matters of translation Jean Laplanche and Jean-Baptiste Pontalis, *The Language of Psychoanalysis*, trans. Donald Nicholson-Smith (New York: Norton, 1973). On the issue of translation, also see Bruno Bettelheim, "Freud and the Soul," *New Yorker*, March 1, 1982, pp. 52–93.

27. See Aristotle, *The Poetics*, trans. Francis Fergusson (New York: Hill and Wang, 1961), p. 47.

28. Freud, "Aetiology," *S.E.* 3:205.

1. From Soma to Symbol: The Emergence of Psychoanalysis

1. Sigmund Freud and Joseph Breuer, "On the Psychical Mechanism of Hysterical Phenomena: Preliminary Communication" (1893), *S.E.* 2:5–6 (hereafter cited as "Preliminary Communication").

2. For a meticulous historical study of Freud's medical and scientific background, particularly the tension between anatomical and physiological schools of thought, see Kenneth Levin, *Freud's Early Psychology of the Neuroses* (Pittsburgh: University of Pittsburgh Press, 1978), chaps. 2–4.

3. Sigmund Freud, *[Auto]biographical Study* (1925), *S.E.* 20:12.

4. Freud to Martha Bernays, 17 May and 31 March 1885, in *Letters of Sigmund Freud*, trans. Tania and James Stern; ed. Ernst Jones (London: Hogarth Press, 1970), pp. 156, 157.

5. Jean Martin Charcot, *Lectures on Localization in Diseases of the Brain* (1875), trans. E. P. Fowler (New York: William Woods, 1889), preface. Cited in Levin, *Freud's Early Psychology*, p. 42.

6. Jean Martin Charcot, *Clinical Lectures on Diseases of the Nervous System*, trans. Thomas Savill (London: New Sydenham Society, 1889), pp. 9, 12–13. Cited in Levin, *Freud's Early Psychology*, p. 44.

7. See Levin, *Freud's Early Psychology*, pp. 64–93.

8. Sigmund Freud, "Preface to the Translation of Bernheim's *De la Suggestion*" (1888), *S.E.* 1:77–78.

9. Sigmund Freud, *On Aphasia* (1891), trans. Erwin Stengel (New York: International Universities Press, 1953).

10. Freud, *On Aphasia*, p. 25.

11. For an interesting discussion of the continuity between Freud's early study of aphasia and his ideogenic account of hysteria, see John Forrester, *Language and the Origins of Psychoanalysis* (New York: Columbia University Press, 1980), pp. 1–39.

12. "Anna O." was a pseudonym for Bertha Pappenheim, a founder of social work and the subject of the first case history reported by Joseph Breuer and Freud. The case is recounted in their jointly authored *Studies on Hysteria* (1893–95), *S.E.* 2:21–47.

13. Ibid., p. 25.

14. Ibid., p. 35.

15. Freud and Breuer, "Preliminary Communication," *S.E.* 2:5–6.

16. Ibid., p. 6.

17. Ibid., p. 17.

18. Aristotle, *De Anima* (403b), cited in Philip Rieff, *Freud: The Mind of the Moralist* (Garden City, N.Y.: Doubleday, Anchor Books, 1961), p. 16. I borrow from Rieff the distinction between "dialectical" and "physical" methods as applied to Freud.

19. Freud and Breuer, "Preliminary Communication," *S.E.* 2:7.

20. Sigmund Freud, *Five Lectures on Psychoanalysis* (1910), *S.E.* 11:16–17.

21. Freud, "Project for a Scientific Psychology," *Origins*, pp. 406–407.

22. Freud, in Freud and Breuer, *Studies in Hysteria*, *S.E.* 2:178.

23. I borrow this term from Paul Ricoeur. See Ricoeur, *Freud*, pp. 5–7.

24. Freud and Breuer, "Preliminary Communication," *S.E.* 2:12.

25. Freud, "The Neuro-Psychoses of Defense" (1894), *S.E.* 3:200–1.

26. Freud, "Aetiology," *S.E.* 3:46.

27. For a sharp distinction between somatic and symbolic versions of sexuality, see George S. Klein, "Freud's Two Theories of Sexuality,"

in *Psychology versus Metapsychology: Psychoanalytic Essays in Memory of George S. Klein*, ed. Merton M. Gill and Philip S. Holzman, *Psychological Issues*, vol. 9, no. 4 (New York: International Universities Press, 1976), pp. 14–70. Although I provisionally accept the distinction to emphasize that sexuality is not reducible to physiology, the enigmatic nature of desire prevents us from reducing sexuality to the discourse of meaning as well. Once we characterize the psyche as a textual economy, the language of instinct and the language of meaning are forever mixed. For an elaboration of Freud's elusive concept of eros, see Peter Brooks, "Freud's Masterplot: Questions of Narrative," *Yale French Studies* 55/56 (1977): 283–300.

28. Rieff, *Freud*, p. 10.

29. Freud, *[Auto]biographical Study*, S.E. 20:29.

30. Freud, in Freud and Breuer, *Studies on Hysteria*, S.E. 2:145.

2. Psychoanalysis as Narrative

1. Freud and Breuer, *Studies on Hysteria*, S.E. 2:160–61.

2. For a lucid summary of the debate in philosophy of history between analytical and narrative modes of explanation, see Dale H. Porter, *The Emergence of the Past: A Theory of Historical Explanation* (Chicago: University of Chicago Press, 1981).

3. Arthur C. Danto, *Analytical Philosophy of History* (Cambridge: Cambridge University Press, 1965), p. 183.

4. Frederick A. Olafson, *The Dialectic of Action* (Chicago: University of Chicago Press, 1965), p. 96.

5. Paul Ricoeur, "The Question of Proof in Freud's Psychoanalytic Writings," *Journal of the American Psychoanalytic Association* 25(1977):835–71, reprinted in *Hermeneutics and the Human Sciences*, trans. and ed. John B. Thompson (Cambridge: Cambridge University Press, 1981), p. 248. Jacques Lacan, too, emphasizes the linguistic and historical character of psychoanalytic "data": "Truth can be found . . . in monuments: this is my body—that is to say, the hysterical nucleus of the neurosis where the hysterical symptom reveals the structure of a Language and is deciphered like an inscription . . . in archival documents also: there are my childhood memories, just as impenetrable as are such documents when I do not know their sources. . . . and lastly, in the traces which are inevitably preserved by the distortions necessitated by the linking of the adulterated chapter to the chapters surrounding it, and whose meaning will be re-established

in my exegesis" (Jacques Lacan, *Speech and Language in Psychoanalysis*, trans. Anthony Wilden [Baltimore: Johns Hopkins University Press, 1968], p. 21).

6. Grünbaum, *The Foundations of Psychoanalysis*, p. 45.

7. Barbara Hardy, "Toward a Poetics of Fiction: An Approach through Narrative," *Novel* 2 (1968):5.

8. See Sherwood, *The Logic of Explanation in Psychoanalysis*, chap. 1.

9. Aristotle, *Poetics*, p. 67.

10. Paul Ricoeur, "Narrative Time," *Critical Inquiry* 7 (Autumn 1980), p. 171.

11. Freud and Breuer, *Studies on Hysteria*, S.E. 2:135–81.

12. Rieff, *Freud*, p. 12.

13. Aristotle, *Poetics*, p. 68.

14. Voltaire, letter of 1 August 1952 to Hénault (no. 14163), cited in Lionel Grossman, "History and Literature: Reproduction or Signification," in *The Writing of History: Literary Form and Historical Understanding*, ed. Robert H. Canary and Henry Kozicki (Madison: University of Wisconsin Press, 1978), p. 13.

15. Hugh Blair, *Lectures*, 2:261 (Lecture 35), cited in Lionel Grossman, "History and Literature: Reproduction or Signification," in *The Writing of History: Literary Form and Historical Understanding*, ed. Robert H. Canary and Henry Kozicki (Madison: University of Wisconsin Press, 1978), p. 14.

16. For the argument that the narrative forms of history and fiction essentially differ, see Warner Berthoff, "Fiction, History, Myth: Notes Toward the Discrimination of Narrative Form," in *The Interpretation of Narrative: Theory and Practice*, ed. Morton W. Bloomfield (Cambridge: Harvard University Press, 1970), pp. 263–87. For a clear summary of positions on the permutations of history and literature, including their alleged identity as forms of poesis, see Roger G. Seamon, "Narrative Practice and the Theoretical Distinction between History and Fiction," *Genre* 16 (Fall 1983): 197–218.

17. See Hayden White, *Metahistory: The Historical Imagination in Nineteenth-Century Europe* (Baltimore: Johns Hopkins University Press, 1973).

18. See, for example, Jacques Lacan, "The Agency of the Letter in the Unconscious or Reason since Freud," in *Écrits: A Selection*, trans. and ed. Alan Sheridan (New York: Norton, 1977), pp. 146–78. For a representative literary critic, see Harold Bloom, "Freud and the Poetic Sublime: A Catastrophic Theory of Creativity," *Antaeus* (Spring 1978):355–77, reprinted in *Freud: A Collection of Critical Essays*, ed.

Perry Meisel (Englewood Cliffs: Prentice-Hall, 1981), pp. 211–31. Also see my discussion (chapter 4) of metaphor and metonymy in connection with Freud's theory of the instincts.

19. Sigmund Freud, "Delusions and Dreams in Jensen's Gradiva" (1907), *S.E.* 9:8–9.

20. Frank Kermode, *The Sense of an Ending* (Oxford: Oxford University Press, 1967), pp. 45–46.

21. Haskell Fain, *Between Philosophy and History* (Princeton: Princeton University Press, 1970), chap. 4.

22. Ibid., p. 261.

23. This point is made convincingly by Paul Hernadi, "Clio's Cousins: Historiography Considered as Translation, Fiction, and Criticism," *New Literary History* 7 (1976):247–57.

24. See W. B. Gallie, *Philosophy and Historical Understanding* (New York: Schocken Books, 1968), chaps. 1–5.

25. Sigmund Freud, *Moses and Monotheism* (1939), *S.E.* 23:43.

26. Freud and Breuer, *Studies on Hysteria,* *S.E.* 2:144.

27. Sigmund Freud, "Two Encyclopedia Articles" (1923), *S.E.* 18:239.

28. See Sigmund Freud, "On Beginning Treatment" (1913), *S.E.* 12:135.

29. See Donald P. Spence, *Narrative Truth and Historical Truth* (New York: Norton, 1982), chaps. 1 and 4.

30. Janet Malcolm, "Six Roses ou Cirrhose?" *New Yorker,* January 1983, p. 103. Also see Freud's own explanation of reenactment as a pathological mode of memory in "Remembering, Repeating, and Working Through" (1914), *S.E.* 12:147–56.

31. Several attempts have been made recently to salvage psychoanalytic theory by jettisoning the metapsychology and its pretension to the status of a natural science. Roy Schafer has been most vocal in proposing that we substitute "action language" for metaphors that reify the mind and depict impersonal forces acting upon the conscious subject. Instead of regarding the analysand as the recipient of unconscious forces, the agency of the analysand should be identified with intentions and actions whose significance or motivation he or she may not fully appreciate. For a representative statement of this position, see Roy Schafer, *A New Language for Psychoanalysis* (New Haven: Yale University Press, 1976).

32. Joan Wynn Reeves, *Thinking about Thinking* (New York: Dell, 1965), p. 151.

33. Olafson, *Dialectic,* p. 56.

34. Freud and Breuer, *Studies on Hysteria,* *S.E.* 2:156.

35. See Olafson, *Dialectic*, p. 57.

36. This point is made convincingly in an essay that serves as a counterargument to Schafer's revision of psychoanalytic theory. See Jean Laplanche and Serge Leclaire, "The Unconscious: A Psychoanalytic Study," *Yale French Studies* 48 (1972): 118–202.

37. Herbert Fingarette, *The Self in Transformation: Psychoanalysis, Philosophy, and the Life of the Spirit* (New York: Basic Books, 1963), p. 21.

38. Freud and Breuer, *Studies on Hysteria*, S.E. 2:300.

39. Sigmund Freud, "Analysis Terminable and Interminable" (1937), S.E. 23:248.

40. I have borrowed this analogy from Fain, *Between Philosophy*, pp. 252–55.

41. Ludwig Börne, "On the Art of Becoming an Original Writer in Three Days," cited in Ernest Jones, *The Life and Work of Sigmund Freud*, vol. 1, p. 246 (New York: Basic Books, 1953–57), p. 246.

42. Freud, "Aetiology," S.E. 3:182–83.

43. Kermode, *Sense*, pp. 45–46.

44. Freud, *Origins*, pp. 409–10.

45. Sigmund Freud, "Beyond the Pleasure Principle," (1920), S.E. 18:60.

46. See Carl Hempel, "The Function of Cover Laws in History," in *Journal of Philosophy* 39 (January 1942): 35–48, reprinted in Patrick Gardiner, ed., *Theories of History* (Glencoe, Ill.: Free Press, 1959).

47. Carl Hempel, *Aspects of Scientific Explanation* (New York: Free Press, 1965), pp. 448–49.

48. Hempel, "Function," p. 35.

49. Danto, *Analytical Philosophy*, pp. 234–35.

50. See Sigmund Freud, "Heredity and the Etiology of Hysteria" (1896), S.E. 3:142–46.

51. Ibid., 3:145.

52. Thomas Carlyle, *Past and Present*, chap. 1, book 2. Quoted in Roland Dalbiez, *Psychoanalytic Method and the Doctrine of Freud* (London: Longmans, Green, 1948), 1:183.

53. See George Dennis O'Brien, *Hegel on Reason and History* (Chicago: University of Chicago Press, 1975), p. 53.

54. Freud and Breuer, *Studies on Hysteria*, S.E. 2:262–63.

55. Dalbiez, *Psychoanalytic Method*, 1:179.

56. Freud, "Aetiology," S.E. 3:196–97.

57. See Sigmund Freud, "Notes upon an Obsessional Neurosis" (1909), S.E. 10:153–251.

58. See Porter, *Emergence*, pp. 37–39.

59. Louis O. Mink, "The Autonomy of Historical Understanding," in *Laws and Explanation in History*, ed. William Dray (New York: Harper and Row, 1966), p. 175.

60. Sherwood, *Logic*, p. 219.

61. Sigmund Freud, *The Interpretation of Dreams* (1900), S.E. 4:103–104.

62. A. R. Louch, *Explanation and Human Action* (Berkeley: University of California Press, 1966), p. 27.

63. Mink, "Autonomy," pp. 180–81.

64. Freud, "Aetiology," S.E. 3:189.

65. Aristotle, *Poetics*, p. 67.

3. Psychoanalysis as Science Fiction

1. Sigmund Freud, "On the History of the Psychoanalytic Movement" (1914), S.E. 14:17.

2. Sigmund Freud, "Formulations on the Two Principles of Mental Functioning" (1911), S.E. 12:218. For a summary and assessment of Freud's identification of reality with externality, see Edward Casey, "Freud's Theory of Reality: A Critical Account," *Review of Metaphysics* 25 (June 1972): 661–90.

3. Sigmund Freud, "Metapsychological Supplement to the Theory of Dreams" (1915), S.E. 14:223.

4. Thomas Hobbes, *Leviathan*, ed. C. B. Macpherson (Harmondsworth: Penguin Books, 1968), 1:135–36.

5. Ibid.

6. Freud, *Interpretation of Dreams*, S.E. 4:103.

7. Hobbes, *Leviathan*, 1:89.

8. John Locke, *An Essay Concerning Human Understanding*, 2 vols., ed. Alexander Campbell Fraser (New York: Dover Publications, 1959), 2:146.

9. Freud, *Origins*, p. 407.

10. Freud, *Interpretation of Dreams*, S.E. 5:536.

11. See Freud's letter to Fliess, 8 October 1895, *Origins*, p. 126.

12. This hypothesis is advanced in two papers published in spring 1896. See Sigmund Freud, "Further Remarks on Neuro-Psychoses of Defence," S.E. 3:159–85, and "Aetiology," S.E. 3:189–221.

13. Freud and Breuer, *Studies on Hysteria*, S.E. 2:6.

14. See Freud, "Project for a Scientific Psychology," *Origins*, pp. 413, 416.

15. Ibid., p. 413.

16. This problem is carefully delineated by John Forrester, *Language and the Origins of Psychoanalysis*, pp. 30–39.

17. Freud recognized this difficulty when he surmised that we may have no memories *from* childhood but only memories *relating to* childhood. "Our childhood memories," he wrote, "show us our earliest years not as they were but as they appeared at the later periods when the memories were revived. In these periods of revival, the childhood memories did not, as people are accustomed to say, emerge; they were *formed* at the time" (Sigmund Freud, "Screen Memories" [1889], *S.E.* 3:222).

18. For the case study of Emmy von N., see Freud and Breuer, *Studies on Hysteria*, *S.E.* 2:48–105. For an interesting discussion of the "derived" status of origins in Freud's case studies, see David Carroll, "Freud and the Myth of the Origin," *New Literary History* 6 (1975): 513–28.

19. Jean Laplanche, *Life and Death in Psychoanalysis* (Baltimore: Johns Hopkins University Press, 1976), p. 44.

20. Freud, "Draft L," enclosed with letter to Fliess, 2 May 1897, *Origins*, pp. 248–50.

21. Freud to Fliess, 21 September 1897, *Origins*, p. 215.

22. Ibid., p. 216.

23. Sigmund Freud, "My Views on the Part Played by Sexuality in the Aetiology of Neuroses" (1906), *S.E.* 7:275.

24. Freud, "On the History of the Psychoanalytic Movement," *S.E.* 14:7–66.

25. Freud to Fliess, 9 December 1899, *Origins*, p. 278.

26. See Sigmund Freud, "The Unconscious" (1915), *S.E.* 14:161–204.

27. Jean Laplanche and Jean-Baptiste Pontalis, "Fantasy and the Origins of Sexuality," *International Journal of Psychoanalysis* 49 (1968): 7.

28. Sigmund Freud, "From the History of an Infantile Neurosis" (1918), *S.E.* 17:17–18.

29. Ibid., p. 13.

30. Ibid., p. 49.

31. Ibid., p. 31.

32. Ibid., p. 25.

33. Ibid., p. 33.

34. Ibid., p. 34.

35. Jonathan Culler, "Fabula and Sjuzhet in the Analysis of Narrative," *Poetics Today* 1 (no. 3, Spring 1980): 33.

36. See Peter Brooks, "Fictions of the Wolfman: Freud and Narrative Understanding," *Diacritics* 9 (1979): 76.

37. See Carroll, "Freud and the Myth of the Origin."
38. Freud, "From the History of an Infantile Neurosis," *S.E.* 17:36.
39. Ibid., 17:51.
40. Ibid., 17:56.
41. Culler, "Fabula," p. 34.
42. Freud, "From the History of an Infantile Neurosis," *S.E.* 17:58.
43. Carroll, "Freud and the Myth," p. 523.
44. Brooks, "Fictions," p. 78.
45. See Culler, "Fabula," p. 34.
46. Freud, "From the History of an Infantile Neurosis," *S.E.* 17:99.
47. Ibid.
48. Sigmund Freud, *Totem and Taboo* (1912–13), *S.E.* 13:161.
49. Ibid., 13:161.
50. For a discussion of the deferred origin as it circulates within the structure of discourse, see Jacques Derrida, "Structure, Sign, and Play in the Discourse of the Human Sciences," in *The Structuralist Controversy: The Languages of Criticism and the Sciences of Man,* ed. Richard Macksey and Eugenio Donato (Baltimore: Johns Hopkins University Press, 1972); also see Derrida's "Freud and the Scene of Writing," in *Writing and Difference,* trans. Alan Bass (Chicago: University of Chicago Press, 1978).
51. Frederic Jameson, *The Prison-House of Language: A Critical Account of Structuralism and Russian Formalism* (Princeton: Princeton University Press, 1972), p. 172.
52. Though critical of Freud's theory, Merleau-Ponty acknowledged the contribution made by psychoanalysis to an archaeology of the subject which reaches latent content beyond the limits of phenomenology: "Since our philosophy has given us no better way to express the *intemporal,* that *indestructible* element in us which, says Freud, is the unconscious itself, perhaps we should continue calling it the unconscious—so long as we do not forget that the word is the index of an enigma—because the term retains, like the algae or the stone that one drags up, something of the sea from which it is taken" (Maurice Merleau-Ponty, "Preface to Hesnard's *L'Oeuvre de Freud,*" trans. and ed. Alden L. Fischer, in *The Essential Writings of Merleau-Ponty* [New York: Harcourt, Brace and World, 1969], p. 86).

4. History and Historicality in Psychoanalysis

1. Friedrich Nietzsche, *The Use and Abuse of History,* trans. Adrian Collins (New York: Bobbs-Merrill, 1957), p. 5.

2. Ibid., p. 6.
3. Ibid.
4. Ibid., p. 5.
5. Martin Heidegger, *Being and Time*, trans. John Macquarrie and Edward Robinson (New York: Harper and Row, 1962), p. 428.
6. Ibid., pp. 424–55.
7. See Peter Brooks, "Freud's Masterplot: Questions of Narrative," *Yale French Studies* 55/56 (1977): 280–300.
8. Norman O. Brown, *Life against Death: The Psychoanalytical Meaning of History* (Middletown, Conn.: Wesleyan University Press, 1959), p. 16.
9. Ibid., p. 19.
10. Sigmund Freud, "A Difficulty in the Path of Psychoanalysis" (1917), *S.E.* 17:137–44.
11. Freud, "Beyond the Pleasure Principle," pp. 42–43.
12. See Brown, *Life*, pp. 87–109.
13. Ibid., p. 84.
14. See Rieff, *Freud*; chap. 6.
15. Freud, *Moses and Monotheism*, *S.E.* 23:125.
16. Sigmund Freud, "The Question of Lay Analysis" (1926), *S.E.* 20:212.
17. Rieff, *Freud*, p. 223.
18. Ibid., p. 217.
19. Ibid., p. 219.
20. Ibid., p. 237.
21. Ibid., p. 238.
22. Kenneth Burke, "Freud—and the Analysis of Poetry," *American Journal of Sociology* 45 (1939), p. 397, reprinted in Perry Meisel (ed.), *Freud* (Englewood Cliffs, N.J.: Prentice-Hall, 1981), pp. 73–94.
23. For a summary of the various meanings of "instinct" in Freud's writings, see J. Laplanche and J. B. Pontalis, *The Language of Psychoanalysis*, trans. Donald Nicholson Smith (New York: Norton, 1973), pp. 213–17.
24. Ibid.
25. Freud, "The Unconscious," *S.E.* 14:177.
26. Sigmund Freud, *New Introductory Lectures on Psychoanalysis* (1933), *S.E.* 22:95.
27. Ricoeur, *Freud and Philosophy*, p. 137. For an interesting treatment of the mind-body problem in Freud's theory of the instincts, also see Stan Draenos, *Freud's Odyssey: Psychoanalysis and the End of Metaphysics* (New Haven: Yale University Press, 1982).
28. Ricoeur, *Freud and Philosophy*, p. 142.

29. For a clear and concise explanation of Freud's theoretical models, see Martin Kalin, *The Utopian Flight from Unhappiness: Freud against Marx on Social Progress* (Chicago: Nelson-Hall, 1974), pp. 125–40.

30. See Freud, "The Unconscious," *S.E.* 14:166–204.

31. Sigmund Freud, *The Ego and the Id* (1923), *S.E.* 19:56.

32. For a provocative discussion of Freud's alleged instinctual monism, see Kalin, *Utopian Flight*, pp. 171–82.

33. For his most detailed and systematic discussion of drive components, see Freud, *Three Essays on the Theory of Sexuality* (1905), *S.E.* 7:125–231.

34. Freud, "Beyond the Pleasure Principle," *S.E.* 18:18.

35. Ibid., 18:59.

36. Ibid., 18:35.

37. Ibid., 18:36.

38. William McDougall, *Psychoanalysis and Social Psychology* (London: Methuen, 1936). Cited in Frank J. Sulloway, *Freud: Biologist of the Mind* (New York: Basic Books, 1979), p. 394.

39. Ernest Jones, *The Life and Work of Sigmund Freud*, vol. 3, p. 277; Ernest Becker, *Denial of Death* (New York: Free Press, 1973), p. 79. Cited in Sulloway, *Freud*, p. 394.

40. Freud, "Beyond the Pleasure Principle," *S.E.* 18:59.

41. See Brooks, "Freud's Masterplot," pp. 280–300.

42. Ibid., p. 289.

43. Jean-Paul Sartre, *Les Mots* (Paris: Gallimard, 1968), p. 71. Cited in Brooks, "Freud's Masterplot," p. 284.

44. Freud, letter to Zweig, 31 May 1936, in *The Letters of Sigmund Freud and Arnold Zweig*, ed. Ernst Freud, trans. Elaine and William Robson Scott (New York: Harcourt Brace Jovanovich, Harvest Books, 1970), p. 137.

45. Freud, *Interpretation of Dreams*, *S.E.* 4:613.

46. Jean-Paul Sartre, *Nausea*, trans. Lloyd Alexander (New York: New Directions, 1964), p. 13.

47. Ibid., p. 39–40.

48. Brooks, "Freud's Masterplot," p. 295.

49. Ibid., pp. 280–81.

50. See Roman Jakobson and Morris Halle, *Fundamentals of Language* (The Hague: Mouton, 1967), pp. 69–96.

51. See William J. Richardson, "The Mirror Inside: The Problem of the Self," *Review of Existential Psychology and Psychiatry* 16 (1978–79): 101–102.

52. Anika Lemaire, *Jacques Lacan*, trans. David Macey (London: Routledge and Kegan Paul, 1977), pp. 198–99.

53. Lacan, Écrits, pp. 52–54.
54. Sigmund Freud, "Thoughts for the Times on War and Death" (1915), S.E. 14:291.
55. Ibid.
56. Ibid., 14:293.
57. Heidegger, Being and Time, pp. 279–304.
58. Ibid., p. 280.
59. Ibid., p. 281.
60. Ibid., p. 284.
61. Ludwig Wittgenstein, Tractatus, trans. D. F. Pears and B. F. McGuiness (London: Routledge and Kegan Paul, 1961), p. 147 (6.4311).
62. Heidegger, Being and Time, pp. 306–307.
63. Ibid., pp. 372–73.
64. Ibid., pp. 424–55.
65. Ibid., p. 426.
66. Ibid., pp. 442–43.
67. Ibid., p. 442.
68. David Carr, Time, Narrative, and History (Bloomington: Indiana University Press, 1986), pp. 88–89.
69. Paul Ricoeur, "Narrative Time," Critical Inquiry 7 (Autumn 1980): 183.
70. David Carr presents a thorough and persuasive argument that narrative, far from imposing order on events, is embedded in the human experience of reality. See Time, Narrative, and History, especially pp. 45–72.
71. Ibid., pp. 180–90.
72. Ibid., p. 466. Also see Heidegger's discussion of temporality in The Basic Problems of Phenomenology, trans. Albert Hofstadter (Bloomington: Indiana University Press, 1982), pp. 256–61.

5. Freud Analyzed: A Philosophical Appraisal

1. Lewis Coser, "Presidential Address: Two Methods in Search of a Substance," American Sociological Review 40 (1975): 698.
2. Marshall Edelson, Hypothesis and Evidence in Psychoanalysis (Chicago: University of Chicago Press, 1984), p. 40.
3. This point is forcefully argued by Michael Polanyi. See his Personal Knowledge (Chicago: University of Chicago Press, 1962), especially chaps. 8–11.
4. Charles Taylor, "Peaceful Coexistence in Psychology," Social Research 40 (Spring 1973): 60–61. Reprinted in Human Agency and Lan-

guage: Philosophical Papers I (Cambridge: Cambridge University Press, 1985), pp. 117–38.

5. Charles Taylor, "Interpretation and the Sciences of Man," Review of Metaphysics 25 (September 1971): 14, reprinted in Philosophy and the Sciences of Man: Philosophical Papers II (Cambridge: Cambridge University Press, 1985), p. 24.

6. Oliver Sacks, The Man Who Mistook His Wife for a Hat (New York: Summit Books, 1985), pp. 18–19.

7. Taylor, "Interpretation," p. 24.

8. Ibid.

9. Richard Rorty, Philosophy and the Mirror of Nature (Princeton: Princeton University Press, 1979), p. 355.

10. See Michael Polanyi, The Study of Man (Chicago: University of Chicago Press, 1959), pp. 31–33.

11. Ludwig Wittgenstein makes this point when he objects to a single ideal of exactness. See his Philosophical Investigations, 3rd ed., trans. G. E. M. Anscombe (New York: Macmillan, 1968), p. 42e.

12. For an example of punning connections that cannot bear the theoretical weight of psychoanalysis, see Louch's discussion of the "Signorelli" case in Explanation, p. 24.

13. Jürgen Habermas, Knowledge and Human Interests, trans. Jeremy Shapiro (Boston: Beacon, 1971), pp. 243–73.

14. For the opposing argument that Keplerian astronomy and psychoanalysis are comparable as ideographic scientific theories, see Clark Glymour, "Freud, Kepler, and the Clinical Evidence," in Philosophical Essays on Freud, ed. Richard Wollheim and James Hopkins (Cambridge: Cambridge University Press, 1982), pp. 12–31.

15. Freud, New Introductory Lectures, S.E. 22:156.

16. Freud, " A Difficulty in the Path," S.E. 17:142–43.

17. Shoshona Felman, "Psychoanalysis and Education: Teaching Terminable and Interminable," Yale French Studies 63 (1982): 22.

18. Freud, "Analysis Terminable and Interminable," S.E. 23:248.

19. Freud, New Introductory Lectures, S.E. 22:149.

20. Plato, Meno, in The Collected Dialogues of Plato, ed. Edith Hamilton and Huntington Cairns, trans. W. K. C. Guthrie (Princeton: Princeton University Press, Bollingen Series 71, 1961), p. 354 (70a).

21. Ibid., pp. 355–56 (73a–d).

22. Ibid., p. 355 (72b).

23. Plato, Meno, p. 359 (76d).

24. Sigmund Freud, " 'Wild' Psycho-analysis" (1910), S.E. 11:255.

25. Shoshona Felman, "Psychoanalysis and Education" p. 30.

26. Plato, Meno, pp. 365–70 (82b–85b).

27. The application of Wittgenstein's later philosophy of language to the grammar of concepts in Plato's *Meno* can be found in John Danford, *Wittgenstein and Political Philosophy* (Chicago: University of Chicago Press, 1978), pp. 155–89. My reading owes much to Danford's interpretation of the dialogue.

28. Ibid., p. 381 (97d–98a).

29. Felman, "Psychoanalysis," p. 38.

30. Jacques Lacan, *Le Seminaire, livre II: Le moi dans la theorie de Freud et dans la technique de lay psychoanalyse* (Paris: Seuil, 1978), cited and trans. by Shoshona Felman in "Psychoanalysis," p. 43.

Selected Bibliography

Agosta, Louis. "Intersecting Languages in Psychoanalysis and Philosophy." *International Journal of Psychoanalytic Psychotherapy* 5 (1976): 507–33.

Aristotle. *The Poetics*. Translated by Francis Fergusson. New York: Hill and Wang, 1961.

Augustine. *The Confessions*. 8th edition. Translated by R. S. Pine. Baltimore: Penguin Books, 1974.

Bakan, David. *Sigmund Freud and the Jewish Mystical Tradition*. Boston: Beacon Press, 1975.

Barzun, Jacques. *Clio and the Doctors: Psycho-History, Quanto-History, and History*. Chicago: University of Chicago Press, 1974.

Bennett, Jonathan. *Rationality*. London: Routledge and Kegan Paul, 1964.

Berthoff, Warner. "Fiction, History, Myth: Notes Toward the Discrimination of Narrative Form." In *The Interpretation of Narrative: Theory and Practice*. Edited by Morton W. Bloomfield. Cambridge: Harvard University Press, 1970.

Bettelheim, Bruno. "Freud and the Soul." *New Yorker*, March 1, 1982: 52–93.

Bloom, Harold. "Freud and the Poetic Sublime: A Catastrophic Theory of Creativity." *Antaeus* (Spring 1978): 355–77. Reprinted in *Freud: A Collection of Critical Essays*. Edited by Perry Meisel. Englewood Cliffs, N.J.: Prentice-Hall, 1981.

Brett, R. L. *Fancy and Imagination*. London: Methuen, 1969.

Brooks, Peter. "Fictions of the Wolfman: Freud and Narrative Understanding." *Diacritics* 9 (1979): 72–81.

_____. "Freud's Masterplot: Questions of Narrative." *Yale French Studies* 55/56 (1977): 280–300.

Brown, Norman O. *Life against Death: The Psychoanalytic Meaning of History*. Middletown: Wesleyan University Press, 1959.

Brown, Peter. *Augustine of Hippo: A Biography*. Berkeley: University of California Press, 1969.

Burke, Kenneth. "Freud—and the Analysis of Poetry." *American Journal of Sociology* 45 (1939): 391–417. Reprinted in *Freud: A Collection of Critical Essays*. Edited by Perry Meisel. Englewood Cliffs, N.J.: Prentice-Hall, 1981.

————. *The Rhetoric of Religion: Studies in Logology*. Berkeley: University of California Press, 1970.

Burtt, Edwin Arthur. *The Metaphysical Foundations of Modern Science*. Revised edition. Garden City, N.Y.: Doubleday, Anchor Books, 1954.

Carr, David. *Time, Narrative, and History*. Bloomington: University of Indiana Press, 1986.

Carroll, David. "Freud and the Myth of the Origin." *New Literary History* 6 (1975): 513–28.

Casey, Edward. "Freud's Theory of Reality: A Critical Account." *Review of Metaphysics* 25 (June 1972): 661–90.

Coser, Lewis. "Presidential Address: Two Methods in Search of a Substance," *American Sociological Review* 40 (1975): 691–700.

Crews, Frederick. "Analysis Terminable." *Commentary* 70 (July 1980): 25–34.

Culler, Jonathan. "Fabula and Sjuzhet in the Analysis of Narrative." *Poetics Today* 1, no. 3 (Spring 1980): 27–37.

————. *The Pursuit of Signs*. Ithaca: Cornell University Press, 1981.

Dalbiez, Roland. *Psychoanalytic Method and the Doctrine of Freud*. 2 vols. Translated from the French by T. F. Lindsay. London: Longmans, Green, 1948.

Danford, John W. *Wittgenstein and Political Philosophy*. Chicago: University of Chicago Press, 1978.

Danto, Arthur C. *Analytical Philosophy of History*. Cambridge: Cambridge University Press, 1965.

————. "Freudian Explanations and the Language of the Unconscious." In *Psychoanalysis and Language*. Edited by Joseph Smith. New Haven: Yale University Press, 1978.

————. "Historical Language and Historical Reality." *Review of Metaphysics* 27 (December 1973): 219–51.

Descartes, René. *Discourse on Method*. Translated by Laurence Lafleur. New York: Bobbs-Merrill, 1977.

Derrida, Jacques. "Freud and the Scene of Writing." In *Writing and*

Difference. Translated by Alan Bass. Chicago: University of Chicago Press, 1978.

_____. "Structure, Sign, and Play in the Discourse of the Human Sciences." In *The Structuralist Controversy: The Languages of Criticism and the Sciences of Man.* Edited by Richard Macksey and Eugenio Donato. Baltimore: Johns Hopkins University Press, 1972.

Draenos, Stan. *Freud's Odyssey: Psychoanalysis and the End of Metaphysics.* New Haven: Yale University Press, 1982.

Dray, W. H. "On the Nature and Role of Narrative in Historiography." *History and Theory* 10 (1971): 153–71.

_____. *Philosophical Analysis and History.* New York: Harper and Row, 1966.

Edelson, Marshall. *Hypothesis and Evidence in Psychoanalysis.* Chicago: University of Chicago Press, 1984.

Ellenberger, Henri. *The Discovery of the Unconscious.* New York: Basic Books, 1970.

Eagle, Morris N. "Critical Notice: A. Grünbaum's The Foundations of Psychoanalysis: A Philosophical Critique." *Philosophy of Science* 53 (1986): 65–88.

Fain, Haskell. *Between Philosophy and History.* Princeton: Princeton University Press, 1970.

Fancher, Raymond E. *Psychoanalytic Psychology.* New York: Norton, 1973.

Felman, Shoshona. "Psychoanalysis and Education: Teaching Terminable and Interminable." *Yale French Studies* 63 (1982): 21–44.

Fingarette, Herbert. *The Self in Transformation: Psychoanalysis, Philosophy, and the Life of the Spirit.* New York: Basic Books, 1963.

Forrester, John. *Language and the Origins of Psychoanalysis.* New York: Columbia University Press, 1980.

Freud, Sigmund. *The Freud/Jung Letters: The Correspondence between Freud and C. G. Jung.* Edited by William McGuire. Translated by Ralph Manheim and R. F. C. Hull. Bollingen Series 94. Princeton: Princeton University Press, 1974.

_____. *Gesammelte Werke.* 18 vols. Edited by Anna Freud with the collaboration of Marie Bonaparte. Vols. 1–17, London: Imago Publishing, 1940–52; vol. 18, Frankfurt am Main: S. Fischer, 1968.

_____. *The Letters of Freud and Arnold Zweig.* Edited by Ernst Freud. Translated by Elaine and William Robson-Scott. New York: Harcourt Brace Jovanovich, 1970.

_____. *Letters of Sigmund Freud.* Translated by Tania and James Stern; edited by Ernst Jones. London: Hogarth Press, 1970.

————. *On Aphasia*. 1891. Translated by Erwin Stengel. New York: International Universities Press, 1953.

————. *The Origins of Psychoanalysis: Letters to Wilhelm Fliess, Drafts, and Notes (1887–1902)*. Edited by Marie Bonaparte, Anna Freud, and Ernst Kris. Translated by Eric Mosbacher and James Strachey. New York: Basic Books, 1954.

————. *Psychoanalysis and Faith: The Letters of Sigmund Freud and Lou Andreas Salome: Letters*. Edited by Ernst Pfeiffer. Translated by William and Elaine Robson-Scott. New York: Harcourt Brace Jovanovich, 1972.

————. *A Psycho-Analytic Dialogue: The Letters of Sigmund Freud and Karl Abraham 1907–1926*. Edited by Hilda C. Abraham and Ernst L. Freud. Translated by Bernard Marsh and Hilda C. Abraham. New York: Basic Books, 1965.

————. *The Standard Edition of the Complete Psychological Works of Sigmund Freud*. Translated and edited by James Strachey. 24 vols. London: Hogarth Press, 1953–66.

Gadamer, Hans-Georg. *Truth and Method*. New York: Seabury Press, 1975.

Galileo Galilei. "Letter to the Grand Duchess Christina, 1615." In *Dialogues Concerning the Two Greater Systems of the World*. Translated by Thomas Salisbury and included in his *Mathematical Collections and Translations*, vol. I. London, 1661.

Gallie, W. B. *Philosophy and Historical Understanding*. New York: Schocken Books, 1968.

Gardiner, Patrick, ed. *Theories of History*. Glencoe, Ill.: Free Press, 1959.

Gay, Peter. *Freud for Historians*. New York: Oxford University Press, 1985.

Gill, Merton M. "Metapsychology Is Not Psychology." In *Psychology versus Metapsychology: Psychoanalytic Essays in Memory of George S. Klein*. Edited by Merton M. Gill and Phillip S. Holzman. New York: International Universities Press, 1976.

Glymour, Clark. "Freud, Kepler, and the Clinical Evidence." In *Philosophical Essays on Freud*. Edited by Richard Wollheim and James Hopkins. Cambridge: Cambridge University Press, 1982.

Grene, Marjorie. *The Knower and the Known*. Berkeley: University of California Press, 1974.

Grossman, Lionel. "History and Literature: Reproduction or Signification." In *The Writing of History: Literary Form and Historical Understanding*. Edited by Robert H. Canary and Henry Kozicki. Madison: University of Wisconsin Press, 1978.

Grünbaum, Adolf. *The Foundations of Psychoanalysis: A Philosophical Critique.* Berkeley: University of California Press, 1984.

_____. "Freud's Theory: The Perspective of a Philosopher of Science." *Proceedings and Addresses of the American Philosophical Association* 56 (September 1983): 5–31.

Habermas, Jürgen. *Knowledge and Human Interests.* Translated from the German by Jeremy Shapiro. Boston: Beacon, 1971.

Hardy, Barbara. "Towards a Poetics of Fiction: An Approach Through Narrative." *Novel* 2 (1968): 5.

Hauerwas, Stanley, with David Burrell. *Truthfulness and Tragedy.* South Bend, Ind.: Notre Dame University Press, 1977.

Hartman, Heinz. "Psychoanalysis as a Scientific Theory." In *Psychoanalysis, Scientific Method and Philosophy: A Symposium.* Edited by Sidney Hook. London: Evergreen Books, 1960.

Heidegger, Martin. *The Basic Problems of Phenomenology.* Translated by Albert Hofstadter. Bloomington: Indiana University Press, 1982.

_____. *Being and Time.* Translated by John Macquarrie and Edward Robinson. New York: Harper and Row, 1962.

Hempel, Carl. *Aspects of Scientific Explanation.* New York: Free Press, 1965.

_____. "The Function of General Laws in History." *Journal of Philosophy* 39 (1942): 35–48. Reprinted in *Theories of History.* Edited by Patrick Gardiner. Glencoe, Ill.: Free Press, 1959.

Hernadi, Paul. "Clio's Cousins: Historiography Considered as Translation, Fiction, and Criticism." *New Literary History* 7 (1976): 247–57.

Hobbes, Thomas. *Leviathan.* Edited by C. B. Macpherson. Harmondsworth: Penguin Books, 1968.

Hook, Sidney, ed. *Philosophy and History.* New York: New York University Press, 1963.

_____. *Psychoanalysis, Scientific Method, and Philosophy: A Symposium.* London: Evergreen Books, 1960.

Hopkins, James, and Richard Wollheim, eds. *Philosophical Essays on Freud.* Cambridge: Cambridge University Press, 1982.

Hoy, David Couzens. "History, Historicity, and Historiography in *Being and Time.*" In *Heidegger and Modern Philosophy.* Edited by Michael Murray. New Haven: Yale University Press, 1978.

Hyman, Stanley Edgar. *The Armed Vision: A Study in the Methods of Modern Literary Criticism.* New York: Vintage Books, 1955.

_____. *The Tangled Bank: Darwin, Marx, Frazer, and Freud as Imaginative Writers.* New York: Atheneum, 1974.

Issacs, Susan. "The Nature and Function of Phantasy." *The International Journal of Psychoanalysis* 29 (1948): 73–98.

Jahoda, Marie. *Freud and the Dilemmas of Psychology.* New York: Basic Books, 1977.

Jakobson, Roman, and Morris Halle. *Fundamentals of Language.* The Hague: Mouton, 1967.

Jameson, Frederic. *The Prison-House of Language: A Critical Account of Structuralism and Russian Formalism.* Princeton: Princeton University Press, 1972.

Jones, Ernest. *The Life and Work of Sigmund Freud.* 3 vols. New York: Basic Books, 1953–57.

Kalin, Martin. *The Utopian Flight from Unhappiness: Freud against Marx on Social Progress.* Chicago: Nelson-Hall Press, 1974.

Kermode, Frank. *The Sense of an Ending.* Oxford: Oxford University Press, 1967.

Klein, George S. "Freud's Two Theories of Sexuality." In *Psychology versus Metapsychology: Psychoanalytic Essays in Memory of George S. Klein. Psychological Issues* 9, no. 4, monograph 36. Edited by Merton M. Gill and Philip S. Holzman. New York: International Universities Press, 1976.

Klein, Jacob. *A Commentary on Plato's Meno.* Chapel Hill: University of North Carolina Press, 1965.

Kockelmans, Joseph J. "Daseinanalysis and Freud's Unconscious." *Review of Existential Psychology and Psychiatry* 16 (1978–79): 21–42.

Kolakowski, Leszek. "The Psychoanalytic Theory of Culture." Translated by Michael Montgomery. *TriQuarterly* 22 (1971): 68–102.

Lacan, Jacques. *Écrits: A Selection.* Translated and edited by Alan Sheridan. New York: Norton, 1977.

———. *Speech and Language in Psychoanalysis.* Translated and edited by Anthony Wilden. Baltimore: Johns Hopkins University Press, 1968.

LaCapra, Dominick. *Rethinking Intellectual History: Texts, Contexts, Language.* Ithaca: Cornell University Press, 1983.

Laplanche, Jean. *Life and Death in Psychoanalysis.* Translated by Jeffrey Mehlman. Baltimore: Johns Hopkins University Press, 1976.

Laplanche, Jean, and Serge Leclaire. "The Unconscious: A Psychoanalytic Study." *Yale French Studies* 48 (1972): 118–202.

Laplanche, Jean, *The Language of Psychoanalysis.* Translated by Donald Nicholson Smith. New York: Norton, 1973.

———. "Fantasy and Origins of Sexuality." *International Journal of Psychoanalysis* 49 (1968): 1–18.

Leavy, Stanley A. *The Psychoanalytic Dialogue.* New Haven: Yale University Press, 1980.

Lemaire, Anika. *Jacques Lacan*. Translated by David Macey. London: Routledge and Kegan Paul, 1977.

Levin, Kenneth. *Freud's Early Psychology of the Neuroses*. Pittsburgh: University of Pittsburgh Press, 1978.

Locke, John. *An Essay Concerning Human Understanding*. 2 vols. Edited by Alexander Campbell Fraser. New York: Dover Publications, 1959.

Loewald, Hans. "Perspectives on Memory." In *Psychology versus Metapsychology: Psychoanalytic Essays in Memory of George S. Klein*. Psychological Issues 9, no. 4., monograph 36. Edited by Merton M. Gill and Philip S. Holzman. New York: International Universities Press, 1976.

_____. *Psychoanalysis and the History of the Individual*. New Haven: Yale University Press, 1978.

Louch, A. R. *Explanation and Human Action*. Berkeley: University of California Press, 1966.

Malcom, Janet. "Six Roses ou Cirrhose?" *New Yorker*, January 24, 1983, pp. 96–106.

Mandelbaum, Maurice. "A Note on History as Narrative," *History and Theory* 6 (1967): 414–19.

Marcus, Steven. "Freud and Dora: Story, History, Case History." *Partisan Review* 41 (1974): 12–23, 89–108. Reprinted in *Freud: A Collection of Critical Essays*. Edited by Perry Meisel. Englewood Cliffs, N.J.: Prentice-Hall, 1981.

Marcuse, Herbert. *Eros and Civilization: A Philosophical Inquiry into Freud*. 2d edition. New York: Vintage Books, 1962.

Marx, Otto. "Freud and Aphasia: An Historical Analysis." *American Journal of Psychiatry* 124 (1967): 815–25.

Mazlish, Bruce, ed. *Psychoanalysis and History*. Englewood Cliffs, N.J.: Prentice-Hall, 1963.

McIntyre, A. C. *The Unconscious: A Conceptual Study*. London: Routledge and Kegan Paul, 1958.

Mehta, J. L. *Martin Heidegger: The Way and the Vision*. 2d edition. Honolulu: University of Hawaii Press, 1976.

Meisel, Perry, ed. *Freud: A Collection of Critical Essays*. Englewood Cliffs, N.J.: Prentice-Hall, 1981.

Merleau-Ponty, Maurice. *The Essential Writings of Merleau-Ponty*. Translated and edited by Alden L. Fischer. New York: Harcourt, Brace and World, 1969.

_____. "Preface to Hesnard's *L'Oeuvre de Freud*." Translated and edited by Alden B. Fischer. New York: Harcourt, Brace and World, 1969.

Mischel, Theodore. "Understanding Neurotic Behavior: From 'Mechanism' to 'Intentionality.'" In *Understanding Other Persons*. Edited by Theodore Mischel. Oxford: Basil Blackwell, 1974.

Mink, Louis O. "The Autonomy of Historical Understanding." *History and Theory* 5 (1966): 24–47.

――――. "History and Fiction as Modes of Comprehension." *New Literary History* 1 (1970): 541–48.

――――. "Narrative Form as a Cognitive Instrument." In *The Writing of History: Literary Form and Historical Understanding*. Edited by Robert Canary and Henry Kozicki. Madison: University of Wisconsin Press, 1978.

――――. "Philosophical Analysis and Historical Understanding." *Review of Metaphysics* 21 (1968): 667–98.

Murray, Michael, ed. *Heidegger and Modern Philosophy*. New Haven: Yale University Press, 1978.

Nagel, Ernst. "Methodological Issues in Psychoanalytic Theory." In *Psychoanalysis, Scientific Method, and Philosophy: A Symposium*. Edited by Sidney Hook. London: Evergreen Books, 1960.

Nietszche, Friedrich. *The Use and Abuse of History*. Translated by Adrian Collins. New York: Bobbs-Merrill, 1957.

O'Brien, George Dennis. *Hegel on Reason and History: A Contemporary Interpretation*. Chicago: University of Chicago Press, 1975.

Olafson, Frederick A. *The Dialectic of Action*. Chicago: University of Chicago Press, 1965.

Owen, A. R. G. *Hysteria, Hynposis, and Healing: The Work of J. M. Charcot*. London: Dennis Dolson, 1971.

Plato. *The Meno*. In *The Collected Dialogues of Plato*. Edited by Edith Hamilton and Huntington Cairns. Translated by W. K. C. Guthrie. Princeton: Princeton University Press, Bollingen Series 71, 1961.

Pletsch, Carl. "Freud's Case Studies." *Partisan Review* 1 (1982): 101–18.

Polanyi, Michael. *Personal Knowledge: Towards a Post-Critical Philosophy*. Chicago: University of Chicago Press, 1962.

――――. *The Study of Man*. Chicago: University of Chicago Press, 1959.

Popper, Karl. *Conjectures and Refutations: The Growth of Scientific Knowledge*. New York: Basic Books, 1963.

Porter, Dale H. *The Emergence of the Past: A Theory of Historical Explanation*. Chicago: University of Chicago Press, 1981.

Reeves, Joan Wynn. *Thinking about Thinking*. New York: Dell, 1965.

Richardson, William J. "The Mirror Inside: The Problem of the Self." *Review of Existential Psychology and Psychiatry* 16 (1978–79): 101–102.

Ricoeur, Paul. *Freud and Philosophy: An Essay on Interpretation.* Translated by Denis Savage. New Haven: Yale University Press, 1970.

———. "The Human Experience of Time and Narrative." *Research in Phenomenology* 9 (1979): 17–34.

———. "Image and Language in Psychoanalysis." In *Psychoanalysis and Language.* Edited by Joseph Smith. New Haven: Yale University Press, 1978.

———. "Narrative Time." *Critical Inquiry* 7 (Autumn 1980): 169–90.

———. "The Question of Proof in Freud's Psychoanalytic Writings." *Journal of the American Psychoanalytic Association* 25 (1977): 835–71. Reprinted in *Hermeneutics and the Human Sciences.* Edited and translated by John B. Thompson. Cambridge: Cambridge University Press, 1981.

Rieff, Philip. "The Authority of the Past: Sickness and Society in Freud's Thought." *Social Science* 21 (1954): 428–50.

———. *Freud: The Mind of the Moralist.* Garden City, N.Y.: Doubleday, Anchor Books, 1961.

———. "The Meaning of History and Religion in Freud's Thought." *Journal of Religion* 31 (1951): 114–31.

Rorty, Richard. *Philosophy and the Mirror of Nature.* Princeton: Princeton University Press, 1979.

Rothgeb, Carrie Lee, ed. *Abstracts of Standard Edition of the Complete Works of Sigmund Freud.* New York: International Universities Press, 1977.

Rothstein, Edward. "The Scar of Freud." *New York Review of Books* 27 (October 1980): 14–21.

Sacks, Oliver. *The Man Who Mistook His Wife for a Hat.* New York: Summit Books, 1985.

Said, Edward. *Beginnings: Intention and Method.* New York: Basic Books, 1975.

Sartre, Jean-Paul. *Nausea.* Translated by Lloyd Alexander. New York: New Directions, 1964.

———. *Les Mots.* Paris: Gallimard, 1968.

Schafer, Roy. "Narration in the Psychoanalytic Dialogue." *Critical Inquiry* 7 (1980): 29–53.

———. *A New Language of Psychoanalysis.* New Haven: Yale University Press, 1976.

Seamon, Roger G. "Narrative Practice and the Theoretical Distinction between History and Fiction." *Genre* 16 (Fall 1983): 197–218.

Sherwood, Michael. *The Logic of Explanation in Psychoanalysis.* London: Academic Press, 1969.

Skura, Meredith. *The Literary Use of the Psychoanalytic Process.* New Haven: Yale University Press, 1981.

Spence, Donald P. *Narrative Truth and Historical Truth.* New York: Norton, 1982.

Stannard, David E. *Shrinking History: On Freud and the Failure of Psychohistory.* New York: Oxford University Press, 1982.

Stengel, Erwin. "A Re-evaluation of Freud's Book 'On Aphasia.' " *International Journal of Psychoanalysis* 35 (1954): 85–89.

Sulloway, Frank J. *Freud: Biologist of the Mind.* New York: Basic Books, 1979.

Taylor, Charles. "Interpretation and the Sciences of Man." *Review of Metaphysics* 25 (September 1971): 3–51. Reprinted in *Philosophy and the Sciences of Man: Philosophical Papers II.* Cambridge: Cambridge University Press, 1985.

––––––. "Peaceful Coexistence in Psychology." *Social Research* 40 (Spring 1973): 55–82. Reprinted in *Human Agency and Language: Philosophical Papers I.* Cambridge: Cambridge University Press, 1985.

––––––. "Self-Interpreting Animals." In *Human Agency and Language: Philosophical Papers I.* Cambridge: Cambridge University Press, 1985.

Toulmin, Stephen. *Human Understanding: The Collective Use and Evolution of Concepts.* Princeton: Princeton University Press, 1977.

Veith, Ilza. *Hysteria: The History of a Disease.* Chicago: University of Chicago Press, 1965.

Wallerstein, Robert S. "Psychoanalysis as a Science: A Response to a New Challenge." *Psychoanalytic Quarterly* 55 (1986): 415–51.

Weber, Samuel. *The Legend of Freud.* Minneapolis: University of Minnesota Press, 1982.

Weintraub, Karl J. "Autobiography and Consciousness." *Critical Inquiry* 1 (June 1975): 821–48.

White, Hayden. "The Historical Text as Literary Artifact." In *The Writing of History: Literary Form and Historical Understanding.* Edited by Robert H. Canary and Henry Kozicki. Madison: University of Wisconsin Press, 1978.

––––––. *Metahistory: The Historical Imagination in Nineteenth-Century Europe.* Baltimore: Johns Hopkins University Press, 1973.

––––––. "The Value of Narrativity in the Representation of Reality." In *On Narrative.* Edited by W. J. T. Mitchell. Chicago: University of Chicago Press, 1981.

Wilson, Brian, ed. *Rationality.* Oxford: Oxford University Press, 1970.

Winch, Peter. "The Idea of a Social Science." In *Understanding and Social Inquiry*. Edited by Fred R. Dallmayr and Thomas A. McCarthy. South Bend, Ind.: Notre Dame University Press, 1977.

Wittgenstein, Ludwig. *Philosophical Investigations*. 3d edition. Translated by G. E. M. Anscombe. New York: Macmillan, 1968.

_____. *Tractatus Logico-Philosophicus*. 2d edition. Translated by D. F. Pears and B. F. McGuiness. London: Routledge and Kegan Paul, 1971.

Index

About the Author

Steven E. Goldberg teaches philosophy and history at Oak Park and River Forest High School. He also has served as Special Assistant to the Dean of Faculties and Lecturer, DePaul University, where he earned his doctorate in philosophy.